BUSY@HOME

By the same author

Busy: How to thrive in a world of too much

BUSY@HOME

*How to thrive through
the covid crisis*

TONY CRABBE

PIATKUS

PIATKUS

First published in Great Britain in 2020 by Piatkus

Copyright © Tony Crabbe 2020

1 3 5 7 9 10 8 6 4 2

A CIP catalogue record for this book is available from the British Library.

ISBN 978-0-349-42928-1

Typeset in Garamond by M Rules
Printed and bound in Great Britain by
Clays Ltd, Elcograf S.p.A.

Papers used by Piatkus are from well-managed forests
and other responsible sources.

Piatkus
An imprint of
Little, Brown Book Group
Carmelite House
50 Victoria Embankment
London EC4Y 0DZ

An Hachette UK Company
www.hachette.co.uk

www.littlebrown.co.uk

Acknowledgments

A big thanks to Tom Harmsen, Febe van der Wardt, and the whole team at LS Amsterdam; my endlessly creative and inspirational Dutch publishers. Thanks for this idea, but also for the years of fun and friendship we have had together.

Thanks to the team at Little, Brown. To Holly Harley for the 'bossy' brilliance of your editing. To Tim Whiting and Zoe Bohm for believing, again, in me and this project; and to Kate Hibbert for taking this internationally.

Most importantly, I want to say thanks to my Corona Confinement Team. To my children Jack, Benet and Seren, thanks for endlessly asking "How's the book going, Daddy?"; for your acceptance of my office-bound hours and for the fun we've had in-between; for moments of joy that have powered me through the uncertainty and urgency of this project. Most of all, to my wonderful wife, Dulcie. More than anything we have ever done, this book has been a shared project. I couldn't have done this without your crazy-fast research. If this writing strikes the right notes, it is because you have tuned my song with your feedback and advice. You are the beating heart of this family, my pulse and purpose. I stand, as always, in awe and appreciation of you; my wife, my life, my love.

Contents

You're on lockdown. Your shelves are bursting with baked beans, bread and beer, and enough toilet roll to last you till Halloween! You've just cooked your first lockdown lunch. Now what do you do?

As you shut the door on the world, you try to keep a lid on your anxiety. Work is going crazy, as everyone stumbles through the fog and fury of a world turned upside down; and you try to adjust to working from home. Your work-life balance is teetering on the edge of extinction. You bounce between teaching, caring, cooking and entertaining. Your children need you, your partner needs you, everyone needs you! Despite endless cleaning, the house remains resolutely chaotic. Your thoughts pirouette in worry. You have elderly, vulnerable parents; friends who are isolated and lonely; family who are key-workers, and at risk. The virus scares you, but so does the uncertainty. You don't know where this crisis will go, when it will end, and what all this means for your finances. While income stalls, the bills keep arriving. You're tired of the rows over money that end in anger, not answers. You're exhausted by the endless mediation between fractious siblings. You're already feeling claustrophobic, and the confinement has just started. As the day spins away from you, you just don't know when you'll have the time to work; and when you'll have the time to breathe.

You know you should see this as a special time with the family. A chance to be a perfect parent. To teach, talk and play tag together. But if you hear "I'm bored" once more, or another Disney song, you'll scream. You should feel positive, but all you want to do is cry and run away. Of course you can't. You've got a report to write, children to entertain and the kitchen to clean, and now it's time to cook dinner again.

If all this sounds familiar . . . read on!

Preface

On Friday 13th March, my wife Dulcie, our three children and I went into isolation. Spain closed its schools and the country went into full lockdown. Since that day, we have been grappling with the unprecedented and unexpected challenges of our corona confinement. Navigating the uncertainties of self-employment, while trying to deliver great work from a home too full of noise. Trying to support our children in their schooling, as they figure out virtual lessons, distant friendships and wobbly wifi. Working out ways to care for those we love, who we can no longer visit or hug. Dealing with our anxiety about health in a family full of asthmatics and worries about income when many of my events have been cancelled – all while keeping positive and playful for the kids.

It was while we were facing all this, that I got an email from my editor asking whether I might consider revising my book *Busy*, reworking it for the covid crisis. "Hell no", I thought, "I've got enough on!" (Of course, I'm not allowed to say "I'm busy"!)

The idea, however, stuck with me. As a psychologist, the place I go to make sense of challenges I face – both professionally and personally – is to the research. It occurred to me that taking a psychological perspective on the problems of this period might not only help me and my family, but it might also help others. More than that, as the idea sat with me overnight, it felt like something I could do, a contribution I could make from my isolation.

The intention had been to edit *Busy*. To cut out the content that wasn't relevant and to refocus the rest in a corona context. It didn't work out that way. As I dived into chapter 1, it soon became clear that, if I wanted to write something relevant, I was going to have to rewrite the whole thing. So, I did. In two weeks! Of course, no one writes a psychology book in two weeks. It takes years of research. So, I have used research, and even content, from *Busy* where I can; reframing it for the current situation. I have also added new research to address new challenges and fresh stories that are more relevant.

This project was unplanned, and like the crisis, unexpected. The urgency to publish it has driven an intensity to my writing that I have never experienced before; and, quite frankly, hope to never experience again! In the end, though completely knackering, the process has helped me, and my family, to make sense of this period. I hope it helps you and your family too.

The core idea

In 1997, Edward Tory Higgins, a professor of psychology at Columbia University, identified that motivation and the way we control our behaviour varies according to which needs are being served. The first set of needs are those of safety and minimising risk; the second set involves growth and opportunity. Higgins suggested that each set was driven by different forms of behavioural control, which he called a *prevention focus* and *promotion focus*, respectively.

A prevention focus is about staying safe and avoiding negative outcomes. It is hand washing for twenty seconds and staying isolated so that you don't catch or spread the virus. It's also about ensuring you don't drop the ball at work and that your children's education continues while you maintain your mortgage payments.

A promotion focus is all about positive outcomes: striving to achieve goals that are important to us, seeing this difficult time also as a great opportunity. In 2012, researchers at Michigan

State University thoroughly reviewed studies into self-regulation, studies that collectively involved 25,000 people.[1] They found that a promotion focus was strongly related to performance and satisfaction, as well as innovation and helpfulness. Prevention, on the other hand, was not related to any of these. There are two important lessons from this in today's crisis: firstly, pursuing your goals does not stop you from staying safe; secondly, if we want to enjoy our collective confinement, and be effective, we need to aim higher than surviving.

This is not a book about surviving. We must all do what we can to stay safe, and all my best wishes go out to you in the hope that you, and your community of loved ones, survive this virus unscathed. The question to ask ourselves is whether that is enough. What if we could look this horror in the face, without blinking, and smile? What if we could embrace the covid chaos of houses over-full, and yet still manage to do the best work of our lives? What if we could take the additional childcare demands and turn them into pearls of pleasure? If we are able to move beyond surviving to a focus on thriving, we open up the possibility of joy and connection; of memories to be passed to future generations. Stories of the time we spent together. When the world, in its isolation, came together.

Busyness at home

As our society struggles to escape the threat of covid-19, each of us faces the challenge of weeks and months confined to our homes. The evidence is starting to come in about the work-life impact of this. NordVPN can track how long people are working, not through self-reports but through actual behavioral data. Their initial findings are startling. Since the lockdown, their users in the US are averaging three hours more work each day! In the UK,

France and Spain, the situation is not much better: people are working two hours more today than they did before the virus. Interviews reveal that many of us feel an additional pressure to prove we were working, since we can't be seen. "At Constellation Software Inc., more than 100 employees got an email from a superior that said: 'Don't get distracted because you are on your own. It is easy to get into bad habits … You know we will be watching closely.' We have also lost our boundaries. As one employee explained, having your workstation at home makes it harder to switch off. "You walk by 20 times a day … Every time you pass there, you're not escaping work." For some, being unavailable suddenly feels off-limits. Since everybody knows that no-one is going anywhere, none of us have good reasons to be unavailable. So we work longer.[2]

In addition to the challenges of performing and detaching from work, suddenly our busy lives have additional layers of demand and stress. Adapting to a life lived within four walls, in a house crammed with people, where anxiety and chaos stalk the halls. Learning to perform at work in a world that's too noisy, too distracting and too tempting; while also teaching, feeding and entertaining the kids. We have a lot on our plates; it's already taking its toll. In a survey of 1,001 people forced to work from home because of the crisis, 45 percent of them explained that they already felt burnt out.[3] It is quite natural to approach all the demands you face by putting your head down and getting busy. I am here to remind you that this is not a smart approach.

Let me start by explaining what I mean by 'busy'. It is that frenetic, racing, cramming and juggling that fills so much of our lives. It is being always 'on', and always doing. It involves jumping from task to task, pushing constantly to do more. It involves trying to do everything in a vain attempt to 'get on top' of work, the children's education and the house; all at the same time! Busy is urgency, distraction, overwhelm and exhaustion.

The opposite of busy is not escaping your confinement to relax on a beach. It is the ability (despite our covid chaos) to bring sustained, quality attention onto the conversations and the challenges that matter most in our lives. It is about embracing the possibilities of our situation and the people we love with a full-fat focus.

However, let's not pretend we started this crisis with a clean slate. The truth is, we entered this confinement exhausted and overwhelmed. Work has been intruding on life for many years. Now, our busyness will be played out in the heart of our families; in the midst of a time when their needs from us are greater. Our ability to approach this period positively, to support those we love, will be determined by our ability to manage our busyness; and this is our opportunity. Busyness is an established pattern of behaviour across our lives and across society. It is a natural response to a world of too much demand; but it's not the only response.

After years of supporting individuals as they grapple with the social norm of busyness, I have seen first-hand how difficult it is to break this habit. I've wondered when, if ever, we will be able to break the grip of habitual busyness. Yet as our patterns of behaviour are disrupted by quarantine, I've started to see this is a unique chance to replace busyness with better habits. To experiment with new routines in order to bring the unfiltered force of our attention onto the problems that matter. To try new rituals of togetherness, to immerse ourselves in the dance of shared attention that adds quality to our time. To explore how to make a greater impact, by deliberately doing less, and pausing more. After all, we can only sing if we can also breathe.

Busyness is a dumb approach to life, work and this period. It is about surviving through ceaseless activity, in virtuous victimhood. It will not help you to thrive today, or in the future. Instead I invite you to use the disruption of covid as a chance to disrupt your busyness. That as you navigate your journey through this crisis, you also guide your life onto a path of more colour, more impact and more joy. A path that is not just about getting beyond covid, but also beyond busyness.

Accept this is not easy

I wrote the original *Busy* because *I* struggled with busy. It was a true "selfhelp" book, researched and written to help myself, as well as to help others. The parallel with this book is not lost on me. The corona crisis is a real challenge for me and my family, as the virus disrupts my work, upturns our lives and threatens our wellbeing. Yet the first four weeks of our confinement have also been joy-filled, and we feel closer to our children than we have in years. We have also had moments that were decidedly un-close, or when the tension or workload has got too much. That has been a big learning too. As we try to adapt our way through this period, it stands to reason that we, and our children, will fail sometimes. We will get angry, we will do silly things, and we will be rubbish. We will not always be perfect parents or perfectly focused on our work. We might start the day with the aim to be productive and joyful; and end it in misery having achieved nothing. At moments of weakness, aspirational books like this can feel an additional burden. A mirror onto our flaws, highlighting how far short we are falling.

How do we stop our positivity from taking a nose-dive after days like that, after we fail? The answer is simple but profound: build your resilience around your ability to cope with whatever happens. A study by Joachim Stoeber and Dirk Janssen at the University of Kent found that the most effective strategies for coping with setbacks are acceptance, reappraisal and humor.[4] So, *when* you or your family are rubbish, *when* you fail to connect, or get wrapped up in busy-but-pointless task-hopping, don't beat yourself up about it. Accept it. We are flawed, we are weak and we are limited; but it is from our imperfections that our uniqueness, our courage and our creativity flow. We are far from perfect but we are enough. Strength and resilience flow not from getting everything right but from getting up from our failures and trying again. So, when you are rubbish, remind yourself in generous humility, "I can't expect to be perfect all the time." Or reappraise the situation as a chance for growth by asking "What can I learn from this?" or laugh about it, "What on earth was I thinking!!".

These strategies of acceptance help in so many situations. I got called away from writing because Seren, our ten-year-old daughter, couldn't sign in to her class. With Seren on one side (anxious) and Dulcie on the other (anxious) we tried to figure out how to get her back in class ... and failed. The only person who could help was the teacher (who was teaching). Rather than persist in our anxiety, and still fail; we accepted. Seren was sent to play until the next class started. It often doesn't come naturally to do anything other than stay in anxious futility. Everything is not going to go perfectly over these weeks of intense confinement and digital dependence. However, if we trust in our capacity to deal with whatever happens, we will be OK. If we go through this period confident that we are doing our best and that, no matter what goes wrong, we will be able to cope, we have developed the confidence we need to thrive.

LIVE@HOME

This section focuses on how to adjust to life at home as covid rages outside. It is about how to set up for a life of confinement in a positive way, with the aim to thrive through this crisis, rather than just survive. It explores how to re-establish routines in our family life because without rhythm there can be no music. It outlines how to make choices about what to do, and, possibly more importantly, what not to do during this period. Finally, it reflects on how to build more togetherness into your collective confinement. Whether you are entering confinement or you've been in lockdown for weeks, it will help you chart a course for a better journey through covid.

Chapter 1

Mindset@Home

Iyori Kashiwara is ten years old and lives in the Japanese alpine village of Hakuba. He was feeling a little sad since his school had closed. He was missing his friends but he was also disappointed that he would miss his graduation ceremony. So, he and his friends decided to do something about it.

On the 14th March, his father Shuhei entered Iyori's room. What he found is a lesson to us all. He found Iyori in the middle of a graduation ceremony! Together, Iyori and his friends had built a truly sophisticated virtual graduation hall in Minecraft. It included seating, a stage and a banner which read 'Summer'. To a musical backdrop, the children's avatars enter the hall to take their seats. Then the teacher enters, solemnly bows to the children and climbs the stage. One by one, the children are called to the stage to receive their diplomas and celebrate together.

When SoraNews24 shared the story, one reader commented, "This will probably be an even better memory than a regular graduation for them."

Coronavirus is restricting our lives and taking away opportunities. It is also placing extra challenges on our daily lives, such as the need to become full-time home-schoolers while continuing to manage demanding jobs. Yet Iyori and his friends remind us, that our current confinement is not an incarceration; it can also be an opportunity, if we approach it with the right mindset.

CHOOSE YOUR JOURNEY

1. Helplessness or control?

In 1967 Martin Seligman, the founder of the field of positive psychology, noticed something unexpected. At times, humans, as well as animals, seem to give up any attempt to change their situation. They accept their role as victims and their total inability to do anything about it. He called this *learned helplessness*.[1]

A sense of control is important. For example, neuroscientist Amy Arnsten showed that when we feel out of control, the limbic system fires up and we don't think very well.[2] However, when we *feel* a sense of control, irrespective of the demands, the prefrontal cortex continues to function as normal, and so we think well. In simple terms, people that focus more of their attention on what is within their control, feel more optimistic and resilient, and experience less stress.

At present, we face a global pandemic that we have no control over and yet it may harm or at least influence the lives of people we know and love, through illness, loss of income, or even cancelled exams. Our choice is how we respond to this loss of control. Viktor Frankl, a psychiatrist, and a Holocaust survivor of Auschwitz said this better, and with more lived experience than I ever could:

> *Everything can be taken from a man but one thing:*
> *the last of the human freedoms—to choose one's*

*attitude in any given set of circumstances, to choose
one's own way.*[3]

The question you have to answer is this: Will I respond to the
crisis as a helpless victim, coping with captivity until it's safe to
go back to normal? Or will I focus every fiber of my being on
what's within my control, and in so doing, approach this period
with optimism and resilience? The choice is yours.

2. Your Covid Compass

If you chose to focus on what's in your control, where might you
start? What could you focus on, instead of the corona virus? Well,
how about addressing your busyness habit?

Use this period as a once-in-a-lifetime chance to experiment
with another way of working and living: an approach to work
that is healthier and more impactful; a way of living where loved
ones are closer and your days are more joyful. In other words,
rather than just trying to survive this period, see it as a chance to
experiment with a life beyond busyness.

To support you on this journey, I've developed the Covid
Compass. Compasses are invaluable in helping us navigate
through unknown waters. It will help guide your path towards
thriving, rather than just surviving.

The elements of the Covid Compass

Imagine the four points of a compass.

> **North:** The opposite of busy is not relaxation on a beach.
> It's the ability to bring sustained focused attention onto the

people and the problems that matter most to us. Life and work are made meaningful by this focus on our core values, great ambitions and loved ones. This is your true north.

South: Great journeys are also animated by micro-experiences. Brief shafts of joy and laughter or togetherness that light up your day and your soul. As an example, I have often talked of the time when my daughter, Seren, asked for my attention as I rushed through the house. I was busy – though I don't remember why. It turned out she wanted to dance. So, we danced. It only lasted thirty seconds before she skipped off, happy. It was a brief, beautiful *butterfly moment* – a flash of joyful connection, however fleeting – that I will never forget. Since then, I have tried to catch myself in the act of choosing busyness over my loved ones. The children help, of course. Seren, who loves this story, often reminds me to dance. She says, "Daddy, remember, I'm the butterfly girl!"

As you reflect on what you want to achieve through this period of internment, think also of the butterfly moments you want to trigger.

East: Life and family-focused matters.

West: Work-related topics.

How it works

- Draw the four points of the compass on a sheet of paper.
- For north ask: What people or problems do I want to give the most attention over this period? What do I want to achieve?
- Capture work-related stuff between north and west, and life-related stuff between north and east.

- For south ask: What moments would I love? How do I want to feel?
- Capture work-related stuff between south and west, and life-related stuff between south and east.
- Now circle the items that are most important or potent to you.
- Put the compass on your fridge or desk.

Let your Covid Compass be a guide for your journey!

A collective compass

Better still, make your Covid Compass a group activity! After all, you are probably not on this adventure alone. So, here's a simplified version to discuss as a collective activity.

To do this, you will need two things:

- Pens and post-it notes.
- A larger piece of paper, A4 (or A3) with a compass (and the questions below) marked on it.
- Lots of chocolate!

Explain to your family that you think it would be a good idea to approach this period positively, and that you'd like to have a conversation about how you all want the period to be, and what you'd like to achieve.

To get it started, share some thoughts on each of the questions that apply to you. Then give everyone five to ten minutes to munch, reflect and write their answers on post-it notes (one post-it per question)

I suggest you go through the questions in this order:

- What do you want to do or learn? (north-west)
- How could your work or study be fun? (south-west)

- What would be fun to do together? (south-east)
- What could we do better as a family? (north-east)

Place your post-it note over north-west and explain your answer to "What do you want to do and learn?" then invite someone to do the same. As each person places their post-it notes, be curious! Once you have all shared your answers to north-west, move south! Answer "How could your work or study be fun?" Continue round the compass in an anticlockwise direction.

You will almost certainly be surprised by some of the answers. Again, capture the most interesting and compelling answers and stick them on your fridge! Why not review the compass each week and give yourselves gold stars where your achievement rocks!

We just got a small gold star ourselves. This morning over breakfast, my wife Dulcie announced that she was going to try baking bread today with the children. Ben exclaimed "Wow! Quarantine can be awesome!"

One thing is sure: in decades to come we will talk about this period. We will remember the anxiety but we will also remember and tell our stories. What stories do you want your loved ones to tell in a decade? What do you want your family stories of this period to be?

3. Your confinement to-don't list

I'm not a huge fan of to-do lists; too often they become the human equivalent of the hamster wheel.[4] However, if we recognise we have some bad habits that might get in the way of what we want to achieve or experience, a to-don't list could be a useful addition to your Covid Compass.

Adam Grant, a professor of psychology at Wharton, and author of *Give and Take* and *Originals* has a to-don't list. In addition to his teaching, his academic research, and his book writing, he also has three children. So, he identified what he should stop doing to make room for the people and things he loves. His to-don't list contains four items:

- Helping everyone who asks.
- Mindlessly engaging with screens.
- Putting work ahead of family time.
- Playing online Scrabble.

Each one of these speaks to an activity which he found he was doing instead of what he loved.[5]

What would your covid confinement to-don't list be?

MASTERY

KJ Dell'Antonia has lots going on. She has four children who, when not in lockdown, play competitive ice hockey. She is also a contributing editor at the *New York Times*. Yet she refuses to *feel* busy. "I'm just not going to let that be the way I see our life." Instead, she chooses to feel calm. What's her secret? She doesn't try and control her environment by doing everything; she builds her sense of control through making choices. For example, she learned "not to try to fit in that one last thing – the 'I'll just empty the dishwasher before . . .' syndrome."

Research shows that what matters isn't getting on top of everything, but building an inner sense of control, despite the storm raging around you.[6] Erik Helzer, an assistant professor at John Hopkins University, who is responsible for this research, explains "The idea of gaining mastery over your circumstances without having to conquer them is an important one." Rather than aspiring to manage everything like clockwork, we should think more like a surfer: skillfully and joyfully carving out a great ride in the face of Poseidon's might. The mastery of a surfer isn't about controlling the sea, it's about mastering their response to it.

The surfer metaphor illustrates the three essential aspects of mastery. Firstly, we have to make some tough, even brutal choices. No surfer can catch every wave, so we have to get really good at choosing which wave to catch. Secondly, the fun only starts when the surfer leaves the relative safety of the rolling sea to dive down into the face of the wave. This takes courage; and they are more likely to fall. We have to let go of our relative safety of doing everything. We might fall, we might even look silly; but we will have a better ride. Finally, mastery happens when we are able to bring full attention to bear on where we are and what we're doing; that's how we move from a sense of drowning to one of deep immersion.

My invitation to you over the coming months is that you surf the living daylights out of your seclusion, and that you use this period to practise mastering your moments.

1. Making choices

Mastery comes from choosing your waves. I differentiate between *inputs* and *outputs*. Inputs are the tasks that come to you from your work demands and family expectations. These include emails, meetings and projects; as well as expectations for household chores, educational requests and calls for attention from your loved ones. Outputs, on the other hand, are the things you actually do. Many of us find our outputs are driven by our work or family inputs. Time and again I hear people describe the causes of their actions (or busyness) from an external perspective. Their activity is primarily driven by the external demands hitting them. This is the wrong approach for three reasons:

1. We have no control over the demands that hit us, so why should we feel held to ransom by them?
2. In this time of confinement, your inputs have probably multiplied, but your capacity has not. Like the surfer, the quantity of the waves shouldn't worry us. We should simply consider which ones we want to catch.
3. Your inputs are unprioritised, they have little connection to what matters most to you, and so are ineffective guides to where you should focus your attention.

Mastery is found in what we choose to do – our outputs – not controlling our inputs. If we allow our inputs to dominate, we're on a path to misery instead. Clearly we shouldn't ignore all demands from work and family; I am just suggesting a rebalancing. The starting point, and primary driver for activity, should be internal: "What do I want to achieve?"

Over the coming months, whenever you start to feel swamped by it all, pause. Take a sheet of paper and create two columns. In the left column, write all the inputs on your plate at that moment. Now, remind yourself of your Covid Compass. Having reflected on that, now choose what outputs you want to focus on and write these in the right column. It is the right column that should drive your activity. Everything else is just noise.

2. Letting go

By letting it go it all gets done. The world is won by
those who let it go. But when you try and try. The
world is beyond the winning.

—Lao Tzu

An optimist sees bad outcomes as being caused by external factors such as chance or other people. Pessimists, on the other hand, blame bad outcomes on their personal failings (an internal explanation).

You are not to blame over the coming months if your work is affected by the daily demands of your children. You are also not to blame if you cannot provide the world's best educational experience for your kids while they are stuck at home. You should let go of your guilt for not doing it all, like an optimist. It's not your fault.

Imperfection

In her wonderful work on vulnerability, Brené Brown talks about how many of us try to mask our vulnerability with displays of perfection. [7] I see too many people tie themselves in knots with impossible expectations. This is deeply unhelpful. Perfectionism is strongly associated with anxiety and depression. It is also on the rise, particularly social perfectionism: the need to appear perfect to others.

We've probably all seen that BBC news report where the professor Robert E. Kelly was trying to discuss South Korean politics from his house, when his young children came into shot behind him.[8] Over the coming months, the explosion of video-conferencing will mean our homes come under view more often. Your boss might glimpse some dirty dishes or laundry. Your children may break into a loud fight while you're speaking to a customer.

If you want to gain mastery over your life, you will have to accept the fact that, at times, a little sloppiness will slip in. You will drop a few balls, or people might realise your house can get messy, or your kids can be noisy. You will be imperfect, and that will be OK.

More than that, imperfection can actually be likeable. Social psychologist Elliot Aronson has studied the effect of slipping up. His studies had people answer questions on video and then do something clumsy. Observers rated the people who were imperfect as being more likeable than those who didn't. This has become known as the 'pratfall effect'.[9]

However, there is a gender effect here. While this book is for men and women, the issue of sloppiness can be particularly challenging for women. Even the pratfall effect applies mostly to men; women tend to judge the person who slips up – no matter what gender – less positively.[10] Debora L. Spar, in her great book *Wonder Women*, describes the intense pressure women feel across all aspects of their lives to do everything perfectly: to have perfect careers, perfect lives, perfect children and perfect bodies.[11] Since across cultures women still take the burden of domestic responsibilities, it is possible that for many, a greater percentage of the additional workload of confinement with children will fall on women. Maybe this is why, in a survey of 1,000 US employees, nearly twice as many women felt that is wasn't possible for them to work effectively from home.[12]

Practising sloppiness
In attempting to retrain yourself to let go, how about some playful experiments in sloppiness? How about playing with not getting to zero emails? Or, before your video call, deliberately make that painting behind you a little squint; or ask your children to build a fort behind your desk before you join. I'm not necessarily suggesting these are long-term strategies but if you're addicted

to perfection, a bit of playful detoxing might be helpful. You are enough, and your imperfection is likeable!

3. Organisation does not mean immersion

If you are juggling customers and children, strategy and schooling, your ability to stay calm, make good choices and perform well are valuable. If we focus heavily on time, we might get more done; but this doesn't mean calm mastery (because you still can't get on top of it all); it means more busyness. A heightened time awareness narrows our attention: We get stuck in the weeds rather than immersing ourselves in the right things. A focus on managing limited time can reduce our intellectual performance.[13]

So, if you want a great journey through your covid confinement, optimize for attention, not time. The search for more and more organised efficiency leads directly to perhaps the biggest blight on modern life: fractured attention. We think better when we have time to dwell, we enjoy more when we take the time to savour, and we deepen relationships when we stay longer in moments of shared togetherness. What is precious – what makes the difference between thriving and surviving – is not how full our time is, but the quality of our attention. Over the coming weeks and months, deliberately build periods of deep inefficiency into your days. Times when you're free to digress, to play, to read or to talk. Times to be slow. Don't lose your moments because you're obsessively cramming your minutes.

PROTECT YOUR POSITIVITY

1. Get the balance right

What's the point of positive emotions? Barbara Fredrickson, a professor of psychology at the University of North Carolina, developed the *broaden and build* theory to explain.[14] Positive emotions, it seems, help us to grow and learn; they also undo the cardiovascular effects of negative emotions, helping us relax and dissipating the effects of stress. If negative emotions are about short-term survival; positive emotions are about long-term growth and capability.

The broaden and build theory was further established through work of pychologist Marcial Losada, a colleague of Fredrickson's. Losada looked at the ratio of positive to negative comments in meetings and found a clear link to performance. Companies where the ratio was higher than 2.9 positive comments for every one negative remark were doing well. Any companies with a worse than 2.9:1 ratio were doing badly. This has become known as the *Losada ratio*.[15] The psychological researcher John Gottman used the same principle to calculate optimum ratios with married couples. He found the benchmark was higher in couples: a 2.9:1 ratio predicted divorce; you need a ratio of 5:1 to predict strong, healthy marriages.[17]

What's your Losada ratio when it comes to current information and news? If your ratio of positive news to upsetting news about coronavirus is less than three good-news stories to one negative story about death and disease, this will take a toll on your ability to approach this period with positivity and energy. More than that, it might affect your ability to support the wellbeing of your family.

So watch just enough corona news to be informed, but don't wallow in the drama.

2. Churning

One of the things that many of us are challenged with at present is the 'churn': the relentless washing machine spin of concerns about the virus, finances, elderly parents or health-worker friends. It's exhausting.

Research by psychologist Roy Baumeister,[18] however, shows there is a straightforward strategy to address this. The starting point to massively reducing your churning is to catch yourself doing it – and stop. Take a few minutes to write down a simple plan of action. What will you do that's within your control? Writing a simple plan doesn't take long, and it's the most powerful technique we know to free your mind from the churn.

. . . or schedule your worrying

Ad Kerkhof is a professor of clinical psychology at Vrije University in Amsterdam. For thirty years he has studied the events and the thoughts that lead up to suicide. He has developed simple, effective techniques to help those who feel suicidal, based on cognitive behavioural therapy (CBT). One of these strategies worked so well he tried it on people who weren't depressed at all; people who were simply churning or worrying. His evidence showed that this strategy worked on people with relatively mild cases of worry too.

Kerkhof suggests we should actively and deliberately worry; just not all the time. Instead we should set aside fifteen minutes in the morning and evening, as our 'worry time'. During that time we should make a list of all our concerns, and think about them. When the fifteen minutes are up, we stop worrying.[19] Whenever we feel a worry enter our head at other times of the day, we tell ourselves that we will worry about this, just not now. In effect, we procrastinate our worrying! If this sounds a little weird, it might be, but there is a wealth of empirical evidence to show it works. As Thomas Borkovec, a professor of psychology at Penn State, says, "When we're engaged in worry, it doesn't really help us for someone to tell us to stop worrying . . . If you tell someone to postpone it for a while, we are able to actually do that."[20] This technique has become known as *stimulus control*.

We can use this during the crisis in two ways:

- If you are genuinely worried about the crisis, set aside 'worry time' to worry. At other times procrastinate the worry.
- You might also do the same with TV news: set aside two slots of fifteen minutes to watch and read the news, at other times focus on what's more positive and within your control.

3. Reverse your motivation

Have you ever noticed that you can have completely different reactions to the same experience? *Reversal theory*,[21] developed by the psychologist Michael J. Apter, explains that these differing reactions to identical scenarios are a result of the motivational state we are in. The interesting thing about reversal theory is how easy it is to flip from one motivational state to another once you recognise what is going on.

Two motivational states that are relevant here are *serious* and *playful*. When we are operating with serious motives, we might be focused on things like safety and goal achievement. When things are going our way in this state, we feel calm and relaxed. When they are not, we feel anxious or even fearful. By contrast, when we adopt a playful state, we look for in-the-moment fun, and we will either feel excited and energised, or bored, depending on whether our motives are being met or frustrated.

Clearly both motivational states are valuable; it's just a question of balance. Busyness can stem form an over-focus on the longer term; leading to us taking it all a little too seriously. The same is true in the current crisis. The situation calls for an enhanced focus on the serious goals of health and safety. We just have to be mindful to avoid getting stuck in a serious state too much, if we want to breathe positivity, energy and fun through the next few months.

It isn't hard to change your state. Four things help me to trigger a change in state: blasts of music, movement (dance or exercise), games and laughter. Actually, just being around children – not in the serious role of controlling adult – is enough to trigger most of us into playfulness. We can all stay more positive by spotting our seriousness and, when appropriate, triggering a reversal into a more present, playful state.

SUMMARY FOR MINDSET@HOME

Choose your journey

1. *Helplessness or in control?*
   Bad stuff happens. We can, however, always choose how we respond. Do you choose to just try and get through this period, and survive; or do you choose to thrive? Focus on what's in your control: you will feel more positive and boost your resilience.

2. *Covid Compass*
   Create your own Covid Compass to guide you on your journey through confinement. North are the people and problems that matter most. South are moments you'd love and experiences of joy. East is life. West is work. Or how about doing this with all your family?

3.   *Your confinement to-don't list*
     To-do lists are dangerous but to-don't lists can be really
     helpful. They serve as reminders of all those things that
     might get in the way of your ability to bring focused atten-
     tion onto the people and problems that matter during your
     confinement.

Mastery

1.   *Making choices*
     We build mastery through exerting choice in our life. Your
     inputs are all those demands hitting you, your outputs are
     those things you choose to do. Don't let your inputs drive
     your activity! Choose to focus on outputs that align to your
     Covid Compass.

2.   *Letting go*
     Perfection is the enemy of greatness. Success and happiness
     comes from focusing the full force of our attention on a few
     areas, and allowing sloppiness elsewhere. Be imperfect. You
     are enough.

3.   *Organisation does not mean immersion*
     Personal organisation and time management do not help
     you immerse. What matters is attention. Through your
     covid journey, don't race and fracture your attention – linger
     longer, savour moments of togetherness in all their beautiful
     inefficiency.

Protect your positivity

1. *Get the balance right*

    There's a lot of bad news around, don't wallow. Get your
    Losada ratio right! Make sure the news you're consuming is
    2.9 positive stories to every 1 negative one. Remember, your
    mood sets the tone in this house, so manage it!

2. *Churning*

    When worries start churning, deal with it! The best way
    to get rid of a churn is to make a simple plan, with steps
    towards your next action. Or, procrastinate your worries
    by creating a dedicated 'worry time' of fifteen minutes
    twice a day.

3. *Reverse your motivation*

    It would be easy to get really serious through this period.
    Keep your lightness! If you are getting too serious, put on a
    blast of music, get up and move, wrestle with the kids. Get
    playful! It will boost your mood and energy.

Chapter 2

Rhythms@Home

Astrid Jorgensen posted a link on her Facebook page when she began self-isolating at home in Australia. She invited people to post videos of themselves singing. Within forty-eight hours, she had received a thousand videos from eighteen countries around the world. The Couch Choir was born. Together, those thousand people sang The Carpenters song 'Close to You' in a three-part harmony (watch it!).[1]

This is just one of millions of musical stories of opera singing out of windows, DJs on balconies and virtual concerts and choirs. We may be locked down but our human spirit still rises in rhythm. These thousand strangers became a community of song, in joyful harmony. They were freed from the concerns of confinement by the rhythms of their music.

CREATING RHYTHMS

What's your favourite song? Imagine you were played each note of that song in isolation. Do you think you would enjoy the individual notes as much as the song?

Now imagine the same notes were played but in a different order and to a different tempo. Would you enjoy it?

The answer, to both questions, is, of course, no. Music is all about rhythm, it's all about sequence. A note is not music; it becomes music when it's combined with other notes. The magic occurs through the rhythm. Studies show that, when we hear musical rhythms, the brain is triggered to produce dopamine,[2] the feel-good reward neurotransmitter.

This preference for rhythms applies to life too. A study in *The Lancet* showed when our daily rhythms are disrupted, it has negative effects on mental health and wellbeing.[3] There is also a link between family rhythms and child behaviour: less routine, more oppositional child behaviour.[4]

Our lives are a little like this at present. Rhythms of work and life, established over years, have been disrupted and randomised. As we try to adjust to a world indoors, the notes of our daily rhythm lie scrambled on the floor. Not only that, into our pile of notes have been thrown the remnants of the rhythms of our partner and children.

The purpose of this section, and this chapter, is to help you to take that pile of notes and create music again.

1. Embracing mindlessness

There is mindlessness in lots of our daily behaviour. Where our actions are relatively reflexive; occurring without conscious thought or decision. In fact, Duke University found that 45 percent of our behaviour each day was habitual.[5] The reason for this is energy conservation.

The Nobel Prize–winning psychologist Daniel Kahneman, has split our thinking into two forms: *System* One and System Two.[6] System One is fast, automatic and unconscious; System

Two is slow, effortful and conscious. Both systems are always on while you are awake. System One automatically and effortlessly responds to experiences. The more energy sapping System Two prefers to take things easy when it can, spending most of its time coasting along. This is a big reason why rhythms and routines are so helpful: they allow the brain to stay in System One autopilot more often, helping us to focus our cognitive effort where it matters most. By doing this, humans have evolved into an incredibly energy efficient thinking machine: only about 2 percent of all mental activity is effortful and conscious.

This works fine in a relatively stable world, but in a world where your rhythms and routines have been scrambled, it can prove problematic. There are two big reasons for this:

- Until you establish new rhythms in your work and family life, you will experience more fatigue and stress.
- System One will latch onto patterns very rapidly, and without intentional intervention from System Two, you might find rhythms and routines establish that don't serve you, your family or your Covid Compass well.

The 'why' behind your routine

Though most routines aren't developed intentionally, they often evolve to serve a powerful purpose. Before creating or adjusting your own daily routine in confinement, reflect on your pre-covid rhythms, and the needs they were serving.

- Write out your typical, workday routine. Do this in as much detail as possible. Give particular attention to transitions: what you did before leaving for work; on your journey to work; what you did on arrival at work etc.

- Now, next to each element of your routine, ask yourself why you'd do it. What need was it meeting?
- Capture the most important needs that your pre-covid routine met. Your task will be to try to meet those needs in your new routine, albeit in a different way.

Then, do the same with other family members. At the very least, ask your partner and children the following questions:

- What do you miss about your daily routine?
- What do you find difficult in our current routine?

2. Building rhythms

If you've ever cycled long distances with a group of people, you'll know about the benefit of tucking into the slipstream of the cyclist in front. We can apply the same principle to establishing new routines. It's much, much easier to build a healthy new habit on the back of an existing one. In doing this, the new behaviour seems to get swept along more easily by the automatic motion of the established habit.

The strongest routines typically happen around transitions: at the start or the end of a period or activity. For example, for most people, their strongest routines are first thing in the morning, and just before leaving for work; starting work and finishing work; arriving at home and going to bed. Think of these key transitions as what Charles Duhigg in *The Power of Habit* would call *anchor habits*. The easiest way to build effective, personal routines, is to slipsteam off these anchor habits. In addition, if you have lost anchor habits, (for example leaving for work) then these are the first routines to replace. Your rhythm needs anchors.

Replacing anchors

The most obvious anchors that you will need to replace are the routines you have for leaving home, starting work, finishing work and arriving home. I strongly suggest you over-focus on helping yourself and your family establish replacements for these. Without them, your day may become an undifferentiated blur, where it's both hard to start work and then hard to stop it.

- Leaving for work: Let's start with getting dressed! For example, getting dressed in formal work clothes has been shown to increase our thinking[7] and negotiating[8] abilities. Much more than this, it signals to you it's time to work. Without this anchor, you might find you procrastinate more.
- Starting work: What is your routine for starting work? Whether it's setting up the laptop, grabbing a coffee, checking in with your colleagues, this anchor helps signal to your brain it's time to work; it's time to focus.
- Leaving for home: This anchor is important to help you switch off from work (see below for more on detachment).
- Arriving home: This is about reconnecting with your family (beyond work and school) as loved ones.

In all four cases, the specifics of your new anchors are less important than the fact that you consciously replace these routines with new ones.

Building on anchors

Once your anchors are in place, you can leverage the slipstream effect for most new behaviours. For example, if you want to bring more focus onto a key project, do it as the first thing you do after your 'Starting work' anchor. If you want to have better conversations with your son, why not build an 'Arriving home' routine, or a pre-bedtime chat?

Think of the behaviour you want to change, and then identify which of your anchor habits or routines you could slipstream.

3. Harmonising the rhythms

Now it's time to create music! It's time to take everyone's needs and create a new harmony for the family or adjust the rhythm that has formed already.

Choruses and versus

Think of your days like a series of choruses and verses. The choruses are the times when you are together. Classically these might be mealtimes and evening time. In these moments, the needs of the whole family are the priority. In many ways, it's the choruses that hold the song together; so pay particular attention to crafting great routines here! In between the choruses, are the verses. These are more individual, where the focus is meeting your needs, or the needs of other individuals in the family.

If you were to think of your family's working day routine as having three choruses and three verses; what would those choruses and verses be? How would you make the choruses compelling? How would you ensure everyone has enough verse time, and that it's uniquely suited for them as an individual?

Drum rolls

Finally, when someone in the family has a moment to celebrate (big or small), how will you conduct the drum roll?

We just had a drum roll ourselves. Jack, our eldest, loves 3D printing. He speculatively wrote to our local hospital, offering to print medical equipment for them, such as masks or valves. He then heard back – they accepted his offer to print masks! Everything stopped at home, every device was turned off, until we had discussed, relived and relished his special moment. Our family's drums are rolling pretty hard for him . . .

GOOD HABITS TO BUILD

Of course, not all routines are created equal. There are certain habits that you should make sure are embedded and reinforced as part of your rhythm.

1. Disconnect

Have you ever held your arms outstretched for as long as you can? It gets uncomfortable pretty quickly. Muscles are great at pulses of activity, followed by recovery. The brain is like that too. Yet that's not how we live. Perhaps the biggest challenge to our ability to think well in today's world is what the technology expert, Linda Stone, would call *continuous partial attention*.[9] We pay partial attention to everything, continuously. We constantly scan the environment for information, messages, stimulation and threat. We are always connected, always 'on'. We don't pulse, we flat-line.

A lack of detachment, from work and devices, is a particular threat when living and working from home. This appears to be part of the reason NordVPN found so many are working 2-3 hours longer each day. People are more likely to 'graze' on work through the evening and weekend, keeping stress levels persistently high.[10] Studies show that when people are 'on call' but off work, the level of the stress hormone in their blood is similar to being at work. So much so, the researchers argue that when we don't detach in the evening, that time shouldn't even be considered leisure time;[11] we just don't recover.

Pre-commit to boundaries

In a famous study, food researcher, Brian Wansink invited participants to eat bowls of Campbell's soup.[12] What they didn't realise
is that each bowl had been tampered with so that, as the person
ate, the bowl secretly refilled. An awful lot of the participants just
continued mindlessly eating; they didn't *notice* when they'd eaten
enough. Ultimately, it was the experimenter who, out of concern
for his subjects, put an end to the experiment.

Do not rely on *noticing* when you have done enough work for
the day. Pre-commit to a finish time. For example, hardworking
consultants from the Boston Consulting Group needed a lot of
encouragement to take breaks. They committed to detaching,
no matter how busy they were. The results showed increases
in performance, satisfaction and career success.[13] The trick was
scheduling this disconnection in advance.

You might go a step further and agree, as a family, when all
laptops are shut down – you could even make it a ceremonial
event each day to signal a transition out of work time and into
your evening together.

Switch off

Brandon Smit, an organisational psychologist, found that one of
the things that makes it hard to switch off from work, is when you
haven't finished,[14] when your tasks or projects are not completed.
However, in line with previous research from Roy Baumeister, he
found an easy solution. Workers who spent the last few minutes
of each day planning when and how they would complete their
unfinished tasks felt more relaxed, detached better and were
more able to enjoy their leisure. This simple activity 'closes the
file' on work and allows the brain to switch off (more on this in
chapter 6).

Creating a social norm of detachment

This need to detach doesn't just apply to you. Your children need digital detachment too. Rather than get into arguments about this, we can learn from Robert Cialdini, perhaps the world's greatest expert on influence. He has shown, time and again, that one of the most powerful ways to influence behaviour is through *social norms*. For example, when hotel guests were told previous guests in that room had recycled, 33 percent more chose to reuse their towels than those who were encouraged to do so to save the planet.

In your family, create the norm of screen-free time, for conversation, games or reading. Without arguing and forcing your children to adopt these patterns, simply practice periods of digital detachment yourself. By creating the norm, they will feel influenced to follow your lead.

Importantly, remember that the social norm works both ways. The US government ran an advert explaining that they would start fining late submission of taxes because so many people were submitting late. Guess what happened? Late submissions rose! So, if you find yourself saying "Everyone is on their phones all the time! Am I the only one who's not addicted?", you will inadvertently reinforce the social norm for digital distraction. Instead, you might have more success saying "If even one of us is on our phones through dinner, it ruins the family conversation for all."

2. Take a break!

Given the importance of attention, how do you refresh it when it gets tired? How might you build these into your family rhythm of work and school?

- Marc Berman showed that when people walked through the woods, their attention recovered better than walking through a city street.[15] So, encourage everyone to take walks. If your lockdown means walks are forbidden, apparently even looking at pictures of nature allowed the brain to recover! So, create a nature wall where you take breaks.
- Synchronise your breaks! When Bank of America did this their profits rose by $15 million. We are more likely to take a break when it's scheduled; and we recover better when it's social.
- Optimize your breaks by remembering the acronym FAME:
- Fuel: eat and/or drink something.
- Attention: switch from focused attention to unfocused (don't just go from email to *Angry Birds*).
- Move: walk up the stairs, do ten press-ups. Pump the heart and your refresh your attention.
- Energy: Get less serious and more playful; laugh or blast the music.

3. Physical habits

Nike's online sales in China jumped by 30 percent over the last quarter for a very simple reason. They helped quarantined people to exercise. Confined citizens flocked to Nike's training apps and while they were there, bought some fitness gear.

Fitness matters for your health. You don't need me to tell you that. We are all missing out on thousands of steps and burning hundreds of calories a day during our isolation. It also matters for your attention. So, get up, get moving and start breathing! Make sure there is aerobic exercise built into your routines. Even a slight increase in your breathing patterns (from a walk up the stairs, for example) will refresh your attention. You might start by breathing better! Linda Stone found that 80 percent of people don't breathe properly when they are typing. She called this *email apnea*.[16]

The default of exercise

A default is a standard condition, like the factory settings on your phone. You have to choose to change them. Defaults can have a big effect on behaviour. For example, economists Brigitte Madrian and Dennis Shea found that when employees had to opt into a pension scheme, only 20 percent joined. In contrast, when membership was automatic, 90 percent joined.[17]

Your family has just lost a huge amount of default exercise: walking to the train, running around the playground or climbing the stairs at work. So, create new defaults.

- Breakfast bootcamp: Rotate who is sergeant major each day with that family member either running the session or choosing which online workout to do.
- Morning yoga: Try out one of the child-friendly yoga classes such as Cosmic Kids' *Frozen Yoga*.
- Kitchen extension: Move your plates, cutlery and glasses to completely different parts of the house. That way, anyone who is setting the table or putting the dishes away has to rack up some steps!
- Disconnection disco: Every night, when work and school finishes, celebrate the end of work with a three-song disco (and rotate who chooses the music) or learn to dance like Rihanna with *Seen on Screen* dance classes.
- You can put as much imagination into these as you want; the important thing is that they become anchored in your routine and begin to happen by default.

Sleep

The brain and sleep expert, David Burton suggests that one of the best things we can do for our ability to think, but also our ability to fight the coronavirus, is to sleep. He explains that the brain goes through a five-stage cycle in our sleep. This involves periods of dream-free non-rapid eye movement sleep (NREM), as well as rapid eye movement sleep (REM), where dreams are wild and vivid. Without enough NREM and REM sleep, we are less able to resist infection. He suggests three strategies:

- Develop a routine before bed, to help your brain get ready for sleep.
- Have at least thirty minutes of screen-free time before bed, and don't take your phone to the bedroom!
- Don't drink alcohol within a few hours of going to bed, it makes it harder to enter REM sleep.

I'd add two more:

- Have a corona-news curfew from 6 p.m. so that your anxiety levels have a chance to decrease before bed.
- Set an alarm to remind you when it's time to go to bed!

If you (or your family) are not sleeping enough, you're not recovering and you're more vulnerable.

BOUNDARIES

We're all hugely aware of boundaries in the context of the coronavirus. Countries are creating boundaries to restrict the movement of people in and out. We have retreated behind the boundary of our four walls. When we do venture out, we might do so behind the boundaries of a mask and gloves. Our boundaries protect us, and they also protect others. However, within our homes, boundaries may have become blurred; and studies show that blurred boundaries lead to increased family conflict.[18] Here are three boundaries that need your attention.

1. The work-life boundary

At one of my events for high-potential leaders, I had a corporate vice president at Microsoft come to speak to us about leadership. His opening few lines gripped the room: "I have never missed my wife's birthday or the birthdays of any of my three children. I have never missed the first day or the last day of any school term. I have never missed my wedding anniversary. I have never missed the opening night of a school play." We all wondered how this was possible while running a billion-dollar business, in a global role. His secret was very simple. He and his family got really specific about what was important for them: these special moments. They accepted he had a big job that would involve a lot of travel; but they were clear that these moments were 'sacred'. Before he agreed to take on any role, he would explain this to his manager. It formed part of his *rules of engagement*. It worked because his family was aligned and because it was super-specific.

Since your confinement started, your work-life balance has become a lot more complex. If you are involved in schooling your children, this will affect your capacity; if you are in a shared space, this might affect the times you are available for meetings. Your implicit or explicit work-life balance arrangement will almost certainly need to be renegotiated. Here are two simple steps:

- Sit with your family and agree what adjustments you need to support them (and you) through this process. Be specific.

- Don't wait for your manager to discuss this or get irritated by your changed availability. Ask for a 'meeting' with your manager to negotiate – specifically – what you want (for more, see chapter 5).

2. The space-time boundary

We have a rule about no technology in the bedrooms. However, we have just broken our rule. For years, the children have used their iPads a lot for school tasks and homework. They do this in the living room or dining room. This was all working well until school closed. Now they have some of their lessons via Zoom video conferencing. Suddenly, they were uncomfortable. It seems doing homework in the dining room is a completely different thing to being in a class, in the dining room. It wasn't the noise that bothered them, it was being seen or heard by us while they were in class. Somehow, Dulcie and I being around felt like an intrusion.

Research shows that personal space is important. In fact, when we feel our personal space invaded, the amygdala fires up,[19] which raises anxiety and interferes with our ability to think. The reason I mention this is what contributed to personal space, and a comfortable place for homework, is suddenly less comfortable for school.

In addition, my office is directly above the kitchen and it has no door. We just never got around to fitting one. It wasn't such a big issue when everyone was at school but it has suddenly become more difficult to work and deliver virtual courses in a full house! It's safe to say that no builders will be fitting doors again in Spain for a good number of months. So, I've had to negotiate times when the kitchen is empty, or at least silent.

None of this is complex, it just needs attention.

3. The children-corona boundary

It's a bit of a weird time to be a child right now. You can't see your friends, you're stuck at home, some people outside are wearing masks, your parents look glum and keep watching the news, and something really scary is happening. We'll talk about relationships within the family in a later chapter, for now I want to focus specifically on their relationship with the virus.

Filter, don't shield

Leo Tolstoy once asked a friend to *not* think of a white bear. Of course, his friend started thinking of a white bear. They just couldn't help it, and not just because Tolstoy had a massive white beard! In fact, Daniel Wegner, who was a professor of social psychology at Harvard, showed that when we try not to think of something, we actually think about it more. This is called the paradox of *mental suppression*.[20]

If your children are young, you might be tempted to shield them from virus news. To effectively tell them to *not* think of corona. If you do so, if you make the virus something to *not* talk about, you will just make them think about it, and worry about it more.

Instead, act as a filter for your children. Ask them if they have any questions. Answer their questions, honestly but simply. After all, you want to be truthful enough so they understand the need to wash their hands properly but you also don't want to overwhelm them.

Recognise and reframe

In times of ambiguity, children look to their parents for an emotional guide on how to feel about the situation.[21] It is for us to manage their boundary between truth and anxiety; and to protect them from our anxiety. Take school closure, for example.

That might feel, to us, like a moment of doom and gloom; a clear signal of the seriousness of the crisis. However, for a child, the natural first response might be excitement. Child clinical psychologist Rachel Busman explains we should be mindful not to undermine children's natural enthusiasm, even if we feel far from positive. For example, she suggests saying: "It's so cool to have everyone home together. We're going to have a good time! Remember, though, we'll still be doing work and sticking to a regular schedule."[22]

However, what about when the news is really bad? How do you respond to your child, positively and authentically?

Recognise: Notice how you feel, honestly. Ignore the voice in your head that says "Even though I watched three hours straight of corona horror stories on the news, I can still be positive with my five year old because I'm an adult." You can't. You'll be infected by the negativity bug. Even if you say the right words, your children will probably pick up your tone or mood. You are your child's emotional lighthouse through this; manage yourself. Catch yourself wallowing in the gloom or your catastrophic talk and maintain a positive Losada ratio!

Reframe: One of the most powerful ways to authentically change how we feel is reframing. Here, you intentionally reframe a situation in a more positive way. A simple way to do this, that stays entirely truthful, is the 'Yes, but ...' approach.[23] Imagine your child has just heard a story about deaths from the virus. You might respond "Yes, some people have died but for most people who catch the virus, it's just like the flu. That's why we're exercising and eating well, so we all stay healthy." If you spend more time focusing on the positive than the negative, you will leave your child, and yourself, feeling OK.

SUMMARY FOR RHYTHMS@HOME

Creating rhythms

1. *Embracing mindlessness*

   Mindless routines have developed for a purpose. So reflect on your pre-covid routines. What need were they serving you? Focus especially on your transition moments. Make sure your confinement rhythms meet these needs too.

2. *Building rhythms*

   When establishing rhythms the place to focus most is your anchor habits. Particularly your habits around starting work and finishing work. Without these you may procrastinate more, and find it harder to switch off. Build behaviours off these anchors.

3. *Harmonising the rhythms*

   It's not enough to build rhythms just for you. The music will happen when you harmonise the rhythms of the whole family. Think of your day like choruses and verses. The choruses are collective periods, the versus are individual. Focus most on harmonising your choruses.

Good habits to build

1. *Disconnect*

   Switch off! Pre-commit to your boundaries: set your start and finish time, don't rely on noticing when it's time to stop (remember the Campbell's soup). Switch of by writing a short plan for unfinished tasks, to close the file. Create a social norm of detachment in the family!

2. *Take a break!*

    Taking breaks really matters. Remember FAME: Fuel, switch Attention, Move, and Energise yourself. Why not synchronise family breaks? This will make it more likely you take them, and make them more refreshing.

3. *Physical habits*

    Build exercise into your confinement. Remember email apnea: it's important to breathe! Create defaults around exercise ... so it just happens. Focus too on making sure you sleep; it will keep your immune system boosted. Build your pre-bed routine.

Boundaries

1. *Work-life boundary*

    This is all about switching off, in order to recover and be present with those you love. Renegotiate your rules of engagement with your manager. Accept that your family needs have changed through this crisis, so your boundaries need to shift too.

2. *Space-time boundary*

    Discuss in the family everyone's needs for space to work and play. Do what you can to give people their own spaces, at least for specified times. Agree when and where quiet time and play can happen.

3. *Children-corona boundary*

    Ask children how they are feeling and if they have questions. Be truthful, but positive. Recognise (and manage)

your emotional state. Reframe bad news with 'Yes, but . . . '
focusing longer on positive. 'Yes people have died, but that's
why we're exercising to stay healthy . . . '

Chapter 3

Choose@Home

What is it about toilet roll?

After waiting hours for Woolworths in Sydney to open, a woman and her daughter took the opportunity and filled their trolley with toilet roll. A fellow shopper, unable to get toilet roll from the now empty shelves, helped herself to a single pack from the overflowing trolley of her rivals, saying "I just want one pack." In seconds they were fighting and screaming at each other. A local police acting inspector, Andrew New, later said "There's no need for it. It's not the Thunderdome, it's not *Mad Max*."

Toilet roll is all the rage. In fact, so desirable has loo paper become that it has required police escorts in the US; people have been robbed at knife point for them in Hong Kong; radio stations have started using them as competition prizes; and an amusement arcade owner in the UK replaced the soft toys in his grabber machines with quality 3-ply!

The theories for why this is happening abound. Some experts say it's a natural response to perceived scarcity,[1] others that it's driven by a 'fear contagion', or an increased need for control in the face of death;[2] or because of heightened anxiety resulting from a new and unknown threat.[3] What all the experts agree on, however, is that it's not completely rational. #toiletpapergate is not the high watermark of human decision-making.

MAKING CHOICES

1. Decision fatigue

The coronavirus has thrown us into a world of decisions that we're just not used to. One minute we're making choices in an attempt to save our company, the next we're trying to keep our parents safe. Then we're trying to imagine a great way to explain long division while learning how to use Zoom. We're facing disease, death and poverty, while we make collages with the children. We're choosing who we can touch while worrying about those we can no longer hug. We all face moments in our lives when our loved ones face major health risks; when we fear for our jobs; when we have to teach; when we have new skills to learn; when we argue about how we'll pay the bills; when our children are bored; and when your house feels claustrophobic and too noisy to think. You just don't normally face all these at the same time.

In short, most of us are experiencing advanced cases of *decision fatigue* and that can lead to stress and burnout, but it can also lead to making silly choices. This chapter is focused on helping you make better choices, with less stress.

From gas tank to emotion

Central to managing busyness, but also central to working, teaching and parenting effectively through this crisis, is the ability to make tough, trade-off choices. I'll explore how to do that later in this chapter. For now I want to discuss how to manage our decision fatigue in order to be able to make these choices.

Making too many tough choices can be not only exhausting, it also reduces the quality of our decisions. For example, for a parole board judge, the harder choice is to free a prisoner, and potentially risk public safety; the easy option is to leave the criminal in prison. Israeli parole boards freed 65 percent of the people they interviewed in the morning, but only 10 percent of those they met at the end of the day; because of fatigue. When we have to make too many decisions, we are more likely to opt for the easy choice, or avoid the choice in the first place.

We used to think decision-making ability, and willpower, was a limited resource, like a gas tank. As we make more decisions through the day, we use up our fuel (in particular, glucose), leaving us depleted, and less able to make good choices. However, recent research is challenging this. For example, Stanford University psychologist, Carol Dweck found that our ability gets depleted after difficult decisions *only* when people believed that it was a limited resource.[4] Other analyses across hundreds of studies are suggesting that willpower and decision-making are not a limited resource.[5]

A better way to think of willpower is like an emotion.[6] It ebbs and flows, but it can also be built. As we get tired, our emotions can often become less positive. However, this tiredness does not have to lead to worse decisions, if we keep ourselves positive and focus on what truly energises us. In fact, as Dweck discovered, decision-making and control can actually improve after difficult tasks; when people focus on what matters for them.

The implication for all of us in this is twofold. Firstly, in this period of crisis and big decisions, we should give ourselves a break! We know that breaks help us to make better decisions. So, if you need to make a tough decision, take a break and come back to it fresh. Secondly, as the crisis tears at our emotions, there has never been a more important time to bring what we love into the heart of what we do. Not only is focusing on our core values the best way to help us to choose between competing but desirable options; they also help us to stay energised in the face of the demands.

2. Where do you want to focus?

Your big 'Why?'

He who has a strong enough why can bear almost any how.

                                              Friedrich Nietzsche

We thrive when our work and our lives are aligned to what we love most: our core values. That is success. We are succeeding when the *reason* we put effort in at work, when the *reason* we support our children, is because we care, deeply. We will stay more energised in the face of the current challenges, if we align our days and our choices more closely to our values.

Which values?

When I ask people to clarify their values, they often ask "Do you mean work or life values?" My answer to that is both, or more accurately, they should be the same. This has never been truer than over the coming weeks. On a day-to-day basis you will need to make tough choices between your work demands and those of your family; between helping your child with fractions or ana-lysing that P&L spreadsheet. To help you do this, you need one set of values for your life, that apply across all aspects of work and family.

This activity will help you clarify your values. Even if you have done this before, the intensity of the current crisis may have slightly realigned your priorities. So, do this in the context of the corona crisis.

- From this list of values, identify all those that really resonate for you (remember, across both work and non-work life)
- Add any values you feel are missing from the list that matter for you.

Delivering results	Fun	Belonging
Energy	Quality	Interest
Relationships	Time	Financial independence
Recognition	Pride	
Competition	Wisdom	Autonomy
Making a difference	Speed	Safety
Stretching yourself	Learning	Change
Caring	Contributing to society	Fulfilment
Progression	Peace	Creativity
Variety	Integrity	Friendship
		Intimacy

Now reduce that list to three, by asking which of these matter most to you, in the context of your confinement.

Values and decision-making

There are different levels of thinking. At one level we can think about very detailed, concrete, immediate things; at the other extreme, we think broadly, abstractly and longer term. In psychology we call this the *level of construal*. At low levels of construal, we are focused on the detail, the immediate. At higher levels of construal, we focus on the bigger picture, in the longer term.

We know from research that when people are stuck or making a tough choice, if they deliberately elevate their thinking to a higher level of construal, they make better, more imaginative choices.[7]

In simple terms, when we are making a trade-off decision, if we deliberately apply the choice to our values, we gain more clarity.[8]

The question each of us should be asking at present, several times a day is: "Which option is most aligned with my values?"

How to prioritise

I was involved with a Microsoft project in The Netherlands with Utrecht University. Microsoft wanted to reimagine the way they worked around attention. The early research, with professors Lars Tummers and Rosanna Nagtegaal, brought a moment of clarity for me. Our data showed that people had real clarity around their priorities, yet they explained that this clarity had almost no impact on their day-to-day decision-making.

I realised there was a missing piece between clarifying values, goals and objectives, and prioritising your work on a day-to-day basis. Values, annual objectives or your Covid Compass need to be *translated*.

Translating your values: your 'Big 3'

Since that point, in every project I do, I encourage people to identify their 'Big 3'. Your Big 3 are the way in which the big stuff like values and your Covid Compass get translated into concrete, immediate actions. Your Big 3 are a weekly thing – you identify the three actions which will help you make real progress in line with your values and goals this week.

More than this, you do this in the context of your commitments next week, and your inputs. For example, one of my values is growth. In line with that, I want to use this confinement period to work on maths with two of my kids, to bring that subject alive for them. I have also committed to write this book. I have chosen to postpone time on maths until after this book is complete (as you can imagine, the children are devastated!). It is this process of making your values concrete, but also contextual, that is so useful.

The Big 3 concept works well, not just because it helps translate long-term aspirations into concrete, contextual actions, but because it's a sticky concept. People start talking about their Big 3. Managers start asking people about their Big 3. Teams start discussing their Big 3. The Big 3 also works outside of the office too. It introduces a concrete language for discussing the prioritisation choices.

Here's what to do:

- Take fifteen minutes of quiet time – Friday afternoon can often work well.
- Think about your values, your Covid Compass and your commitments next week.
- Identify activities that are aligned to your values and relevant to your Covid Compass and commitments for the coming week.
- Now choose your Big 3: the three activities that you feel will be most valuable.
- Finally, capture your Big 3 for easy reference throughout the week. For example, a post-it on your laptop, on the fridge or in your calendar – choose somewhere where you see it regularly.

I will talk more about how you use your Big 3 in chapter 6.

TRADE-OFFS

Mike Flint is the personal pilot of Warren Buffett, the billionaire investor and philanthropist. Flint asked Buffett for advice on life goals and prioritisation. Buffett asked Flint to identify his top twenty-five goals. Once Flint was done, Buffett then asked him to choose his top five goals. Then the advice got interesting. Buffett told Flint to call the second list (i.e. goals six to twenty-five) the 'Avoid at all costs list'. He told Flint that if he wanted to have the life he wanted, he should do everything in his power to avoid pursuing the items on this second list. They were the things that would distract him from his true goals.[9] They were the trade-offs he would need to make.

Trade-offs are the dirty little secret behind all corporate strategy. No company can do everything well; no person has the time to be able to give full attention to everything and everyone they want. It is only through trade-offs that we allow ourselves to bring focus onto what matters. For example, when CEO Tim Cook was asked why Apple was successful, he explained it was because they said no to great ideas every day – but here's the important bit – in order to put *enormous energy* behind the few they choose.

What's true for Buffett's pilot and for Apple, is true for every one of us during the coming weeks and months. Our confinement will be more memorable, our time with our family sweeter and our work more impactful if we make trade-offs. We will thrive through covid if we say no to lots of opportunities, in order to put *enormous energy* into the things we choose.

1. Trade-offs: asking the right questions

So what do you want to do with your covid time? Do you want to:

- Exercise with Joe Wicks?
- Take dance classes with the New York City Ballet's principal dancer?
- Listen to Patrick Stewart reading poetry?
- Virtually tour The Louvre with your children?
- Chop garlic like a pro with *The Kitchn*?
- Develop your Chinese language skills with Rosetta Stone?
- Take a Harvard University course on the Pyramids of Giza?
- Learn to play the electric guitar with Fender?

All of these opportunities are available for free during this crisis, and they all sound pretty good to me.

In their book *Decisive*, business strategists Chip and Dan Heath explain that perhaps the biggest flaw in human decision-making is *narrow framing*. This means that when we make a decision, we only look at the option being presented; we fail to consider the context, or the implications. We ask ourselves "whether or not" we want to do something. When I look at the list above, my answer to everything (apart from the garlic chopping) would be an emphatic *YES*!

This is the problem. The brain fails to take into account the implications of these decisions. The truth is, every choice has a consequence. Each time you choose something, you unchoose something else. Over the coming weeks, I will not be able to learn the electric guitar, teach my children maths, write this book, hold family film nights to watch all the *Star Wars* movies and still have time to earn some money and play ping pong with the kids. I have to choose, and so do you. More than that, it is only when we choose to *not* do things, that we allow those things we have chosen to come to life, to be fully relished in their glorious Technicolour.

A better question

Paul Nutt, business school professor at Ohio State University, found a much better question to ask than "whether or not". His research found that when executives asked "which", they got much better results. 'Which' questions force us to look at two or more options. Rather than looking at each item in the list and asking whether or not you'd like to do it, instead ask which of those options you'd like to do most, and which to not do.

An even better question

In the early years after the Korean War, the American public kept asking president Dwight D. Eisenhower to build heavier bombers. He reminded them that "The cost of one modern heavy bomber is this: a modern brick school in more than thirty cities." Every decision has an *opportunity cost*. Opportunity cost is a concept derived from economics that describes what we miss out on, or lose, through making a decision. The true cost of learning Chinese each evening is that I will not be able to play *War Thunder* with my son Jack. To include the opportunity cost in your decision-making, ask a question I learned from the author and coaching expert Michael Bungay Stanier, "If I'm saying yes to this, what am I saying no to?"[10]

2. Making trade-offs

It was psychologists Amos Tversky and Daniel Kahneman who first showed that we have an irrational aversion to loss. When thinking about trade-off choices, it is natural to think of these as losses. Instead of "So, I won't be able to do my Fender guitar classes?", I prefer to think of trade-offs a little differently – more like an artform.

Picture yourself as a sculptor. The big block of stone you start with represents all the demands and opportunities you have at present. These might relate to work, family, learning, health or entertainment. You will only release the beauty of that stone when you cut a lot of it away. Making trade-offs is like that. It's a deeply creative process, where our goal is to create something beautiful, something enriching. Your task is to look on the demands and opportunities of your covid confinement like an artist and carve out your very own *Venus de Milo*.

I am now going to ask you to think of trade-offs at three levels: the whole period, this week and today. I do this deliberately for two reasons: it helps surface specific and concrete trade-offs, as well as broader lifestyle choices. Starting at the high level and moving to today helps to make it real, and drive commitment.

Your Covid Compass trade-offs
What do you choose *not* to do in order to focus attention on what you value most and on your Covid Compass? What do you choose to *do less*?

Big 3 trade-offs
What do you choose *not* to do in order to focus your attention this week on your Big 3? What do you choose to *do less*?

Today's trade-offs
What do you choose *not* to do in order to make today a work of art? What do you choose to *do less*?

3. Trade-off tips

Play the percentages
I had the privilege of meeting Dutch athlete Ireen Wüst in 2016. Among her many sporting accomplishments are five Olympic

gold medals for speed-skating. We were both on RTL Late Night, a popular Dutch TV chat show. When we met, she said something to the effect that she would love to read my book because parts of her life were chaotic. You know those times when you walk away from a situation, and you suddenly realise what you should have said, but didn't? What I said at the time was something like "Oh really!", but what I wished I had said was "That's success. Success is about being great in a few areas while allowing a little chaos to reign elsewhere." If Ireen had dealt, perfectly, with all the sloppiness, she would not have won those medals.

I bring up the topic of sloppiness again, because trade-offs are not just about doing something or not. They are also about choosing to do some things less well. Not preparing fully for a meeting, doing a pretty average job of teaching your children grammar or serving them pizza for dinner (again)! There will be times over the coming weeks when the very best thing you can do, in service of your Covid Compass, is to give your children an iPad or turn on the TV. Yes, you could spend time writing poetry with them, but if the best use of your attention at that moment is something else, feel no guilt. The point is, we have to differentiate between the things we will do with enormous energy and those we will simply execute as mindlessly and rapidly as possible. Perfection (in everything) is the enemy of greatness (in anything).

Tip: Give your tasks a percentage rating. Ask yourself "Is this a 20 percent task or a 100 percent task (or somewhere in between)?"

Good choices take energy

Remember the parole judges we mentioned earlier? The 'easy' choice for them was to deny parole, the tough choice was to parole prisoners, potentially risking public safety. As the day wore on, they freed fewer people. However, after each break, judges made more of the difficult choices again to free prisoners. We also discussed that willpower and decision fatigue can be thought of like an emotion, it typically drops as we get tired but can be re-energised by refocusing on what inspires us.

Tip: Before prioritising and making trade-off choices:

- Take a break.
- Use your values and your Covid Compass to energise you and help you choose.

DO NOTHING

Doing nothing is hard. One of the reasons that people have been buying so much toilet paper is that doing something gives us a sense of control. We face a scary and unpredictable pandemic. The government, our employers and our children's school are all making huge decisions about our lives. In the face of so much uncertainty, it is natural to attempt to exert some control; to focus on something we can do. So we stockpile. We choose to buy more than normal.

The same can be true of activity. If we keep active, we don't have to think too much. We can drown out the worries of family and future. We embrace the multiple roles and the additional demands of collective confinement, because they allow us to do more, and therefore think less.

1. Alone with your thoughts

The preference for activity over inactivity isn't unique to our current confinement. In fact, professor of psychology at the University of Virginia, Timothy D. Wilson, found that many people prefer to give themselves painful electric shocks rather than be left alone with nothing to do![11] With our distraction devices aiding and abetting this preference, we can now almost totally exclude nothingness from our lives. One survey by the U.S. Bureau of Labor Statistics found that that 83 percent of people spend no time at all 'relaxing or thinking'.[12] We are the first generation who have lived with so little time alone with our thoughts, in inactive reflection. So, isn't this a good thing, especially if our activity drowns out our angst?

When we are on task, we generate input and stimulation for the brain. This information is raw and external. It is only when the brain takes this information and associates it with previous experiences, that it begins to have meaning. This is the job of your default network, which comes alive when you are off-task. Your default network can be thought of as your cognitive digestive system. It digests external data into something more personal – into *your* opinion, *your* insight and *your* wisdom.

For example, where do you have your best ideas? If you are like most people, you would say the shower. This is because it's one of the few times in your day when you are not producing or consuming something. Your brain is left free to reflect, to connect and to make sense. And hey presto, insights happen!

Over the next few months we are in for an unpredictable journey. If your aspiration for this period is numbness, then throw yourself into activity with reckless (and mindless) abandon. If you want to thrive through this period rather than just survive, you will need to adapt and re-imagine with an unprecedented intensity. As our relationships are tested by common confinement and anxiety, they will only deepen if we are also willing to learn from our conversations and conflicts. This is the job of the default network. In fact, so important is inactive reflection, Martin Heidegger suggested it was the essence of our humanity. If you want to thrive through these uncertain times, adapting and learning as you go, you will need to spend time alone with your brain.

Drowning in worries

What if you're one of the millions of people who is self-employed or laid off because of the coronavirus? Surely the benefit of activity is that it drowns out the worries. Consistent research shows we tend to be happier when we're active, even if that activity is meaningless.[13] However, if we fail to spend time inside ourselves, facing our demons as well as our dreams, we can't resolve our problems and make sense of the future we want. We miss out on critical psychological work.

As you amble into your thoughts, be careful to mind-wander mindfully. There is a big difference between worrying and wandering. Worrying is focused on regrets or things you have no control over; and it tends to fixate. Wandering is more scattered, exploring possibilities, mixing things up and asking "What if?" When your wandering turns to the dark side (apologies, too much *Star Wars!*) gently guide it back to options and possibilities. For example, when my wandering turns to worrying, I ask myself "So what's my opportunity here?" Redirect your creative randomness onto the questions you need to resolve, then sit back and let your default network do the rest!

2. How to do nothing (since we have forgotten how to!)

Here are a few ideas on how to build more 'dead time' into your day.

Fifteen minutes

A study by Harvard researchers, including Francesca Gino, proved experimentally that doing nothing improves performance. They were in an environment where they had to learn fast: training to work in a call centre for Wipro, in India. It was an intense two-week programme of lessons and practice calls. One group was asked to work as normal, continuing to take practice calls right until the end. The other group was asked to sit for fifteen minutes in silent reflection at the end of the day. In the end of programme test, the reflecting group performed 23 percent better! We all need to do a lot of learning at present. We will learn best if we create the space for it through inactivity. Whether you use a journal, a diary or just take bath; spend time in silence, at the end of each day, reflecting on what you've learnt.

Do a Darwin

Darwin had a routine of working hard for a few hours, then going for a long walk. This stroll of his was the point at which he let his mind wander as he ambled. Making sense, wondering and digesting. I regularly 'Do a Darwin' and go for a stroll after a few hours of writing. However, in Spain at present, strolling is not allowed. I've had to learn to Do a Darwin in a more contained area: I'm becoming a born-again gardener. I find the low cognitive demands of planting and weeding – if done without urgency, distraction or loud music – can become decidedly Darwin-esqe! If you live in an apartment, domestic chores can achieve the same effect, as long as you amble through them.

Nescafé moments

Many years ago, Nescafé ran an iconic advert. A young woman drove her VW Beetle to the end of a sand dune overlooking the sea. She was clearly upset, heart-broken even. Then the music started, playing the song 'I Can See Clearly Now'. She opened her glovebox and found what she needed to make herself a cup of Nescafé. In a matter of moments she was hugging her steaming mug, sitting on the bonnet of her car, gazing out to sea in silent reflection. We no longer pitied her, now we wanted to be her!

Dulcie and I have a favourite apartment when we stay in Amsterdam. It's a great location; but the best thing is the window.

You can recline on the sofa, right next to the window, and gaze outside for ages. We started to call this our Nescafé Window. Now, we've come to call moments of sitting on our own, gazing out of a window, our 'Nescafé Moments' (even though we're drinking tea).

Where is your Nescafe Window and how could you build more Nescafé Moments into your day?

3. Boredom

> *The gods were bored; therefore they created human beings.*
>
> Søren Kierkegaard

Martin Luther King wrote 'Letter From a Birmingham Jail' when he was imprisoned and bored. If one of the barriers you feel about inactivity is boredom, it's worth remembering that boredom has benefits. It is a valuable creativity booster. It seems that, when we are bored, the brain starts wandering, searching for how to get un-bored. As Texas A&M University psychologist Heather Lench explains "Boredom becomes a seeking state" which primes the brain for creativity. One study tested this by deliberately boring people: they were asked to copy a phone book! Compared to the people who weren't bored, they were more creative. So they took the study further. They created a *really* boring task: reading the phone book. It turned out, reading the phone book produced even more creativity than copying it. The more boring the task, the more of a creative seeking state was being triggered.

"I'm bored!"

This is something you are probably hearing a lot from your children. So, here's my suggestion: don't try to fix it for them. Yuko Munakata, a professor in psychology and neuroscience at the

University of Colorado has found that our children are not bored enough. We have filled their evenings with after-school activities and structured learning experiences. When Munakata compared children who did lots of structured activities to those with lots of unstructured ('boring') time, the latter group had a more developed central executive, the system in the brain which is vital for problem-solving and imagination. My wife and I have a phrase that we say to our children whenever they say "I'm bored!" We respond with "That's our greatest gift to you!" We firmly believe that our children need boredom. It is normally when they are bored that they end up having the most fun. That's when they create new games, start drawing or building rockets. If you take away their boredom you might be robbing them of a chance to grow. You will also be teaching them that it's your responsibility to get out of boredom, and that's not a great lesson. It's their job, and it's important work for them!

SUMMARY FOR CHOOSE@HOME

Making choices

1. *Decision fatigue*
    We all have a big case of decision fatigue at present. Recent research shows though that willpower isn't like a gas tank, which runs out, but more like an emotion (it ebbs and flows) and can be re-energised by focusing on what we value.

2. *Where do you want to focus?*
    It has never been more important to clarify what you care about most – your values – and to bring daily focus to them. Deliberately elevating choices to your values (a higher level of construal) helps clarify decision-making.

3.   *Your Big 3*
      It's essential to clarify values and your Covid Compass but
      these also need to be translated on a weekly basis. On
      Friday afternoon, clarify your Big 3 for the coming week: the
      concrete activities that focus on the people and problems
      that matter most.

Trade-offs

1.   *Asking the right questions*
      We tend to ask the wrong question when deciding our
      actions. We ask 'Whether or not?'; this ignores the opportu-
      nity cost. It's better to ask 'Which?' activity is the best use of
      your attention. Better still ask 'If I'm saying yes to this, what
      am I saying no to?'*

2.   *Making trade-offs*
      When making trade-offs, do it at three levels. Covid
      Compass: what trade-offs do I need to have the confine-
      ment I want? Big 3: what trade-offs do I need to make next
      week to deliver my Big 3? Today: what trade-offs do I need
      to make today, to focus on what matters?

3.   *Play the percentages*
      Trade-offs are not just about saying 'No', they are also about
      choosing to do things less well. Ask yourself 'Is this a 20
      percent job?' Or 'Is it a 100 percent job?' Also, remember,
      tough choices are hard work, make those choices after a
      break. Breaks help us to re-focus on what matters.

Do nothing

1. *Alone with your thoughts*
    There has never been a generation that has spent less time alone with its thoughts than us. Especially at times like this, we need silent reflection. Do nothing mindfully, there is a big difference between wandering and worrying. If you worry, redirect thoughts by asking "What if?"

2. *How to do nothing*
    Build 'Nescafe Moments' into your life: time spent looking out of a window, clutching a hot drink, in silence. Or 'Do a Darwin' by having a walk or, if that's not possible, do low-level activity, slowly. Or, spend fifteen minutes reflecting: you'll perform better and learn more.

3. *Boredom*
    Don't avoid boredom. Boredom triggers a seeking state, which drives curiosity and creativity. In addition, don't deprive your children of boredom. Without enough boredom, their central executive doesn't develop properly. When you hear "I'm bored" say "That's my gift to you!"

Chapter 4

Together@Home

What have been the best sunsets of your life? The sun sets every day, but occasionally, those moments are seared onto our memories.

What's interesting about memories such as these is that they are not really based on the colours of the sky, but the quality of the moment. They are about location and timing, but most importantly, they are about the people you were with.

Which is why so many people reacted when a picture was shared of an eight-seven-year-old artist from Wuhan watching the sunset. The image showed that the artist was suffering from coronavirus. He was lying in a hospital bed, wearing an oxygen mask. Clearly in transit, the bed was on the street, with a perfect view of the sunset. What makes the image so moving is that alongside the patient, Dr Liu Kai, in full hazmat suit, is pointing at the sunset. In the crazy haste of crisis caring, Dr Kai had paused for a moment of togetherness.

'Together' may just be the word that most powerfully captures our collective experience of the covid crisis. Around the world we have seen scenes of spontaneous togetherness as families reconnect in their isolation, strangers help each other, and streets and towns rediscover they are also communities. This chapter is about just that. It's about embracing our togetherness, because our moments are better, and our lives are more meaningful, when they are shared.

Everyone needs relationships

Lisa Berkman is an internationally respected expert on social and public policy, based at Havard. After years of careful statistical analysis she has become clear on what drives health and wellbeing: quality relationships, or, in her terms, 'social connectedness'.[1] In one study of seven thousand adults, those with fewer social ties at the beginning of the study were two to three times more likely to die during the nine years of her study than those who had plentiful relationships.[2] Jonathan Haidt, professor of psychology at NYU, explains why good relationships are particularly valuable in our covid confinement: they strengthen the immune system, and reduce the risk of anxiety and depression.[3] In fact, loneliness and isolation have been shown to be bigger health risk factors than either smoking or obesity![4]

We will not just be healthier as a result of better relationships, we'll also be happier. Ed Diener, a senior scientist for Gallup and psychology professor, and Martin Seligman studied very happy people. They found that the common factor linking the happiest people was "their strong ties to friends and family and commitment to spending time with them."[5] In other words, if we have a high level of engagement with those who are important to us over this period, our confinement will be good. If we don't, it will be bad. It's pretty much as simple as that. This unexpected and unprecedented period of enforced isolation with those we love might just be a gift. We have a chance to deepen our connections; to savour this time, with all its colour and sunsets, in togetherness.

DOING TOGETHER

Our homes and our families are our harbours. A place to shelter, to refresh and recharge. On a daily basis, the family members sally forth from the port. On our own course, doing our own thing; largely independent of each other. Our work and play is outside. At night, we return, and moor up; eager to escape the confines of harbour walls again tomorrow. The harbour is safe, but it's not where the action is; the adventure is beyond.

At present, our harbour is all there is. The storm is raging outside, but we don't need to stay moored inside. This section is about turning your harbour into a lake. Building opportunities to work and play together. While the sea is off limits, we can still cast off and explore; it can still be a place of adventure.

1. Working together

Few teenagers actively look to help around the house. As parents, it might be natural to 'give the kids a break' during this trying time, and not bother them with chores. Is that the right approach? In a thorough analysis of 752 adolescents, behavioural psychologists Eva Telzer and Andrew Fuligni found that helping in the home was associated with happiness.[6] Those teens who cleaned the house, helped with siblings or cooked, were happier. Also, when any individual did more helping, their happiness levels and sense of positivity rose. Finally, they found that, looking across European, Latin American and Chinese groups, there were no differences in this relationship between helping and happiness. Helping gave the adolescents a sense of purpose and connection to the family.

In essence, if we want our children to have a happy and positive confinement, not only should we get them to help around the house, we should get them to help more! (Sorry kids!)

Don't demand, default

As you probably know, whether or not you will donate your organs has very little to do with whether or not you agree that people should donate their organs. For example, while most people approve of organ donation, in Germany only 12 percent actually consent to donate their organs. Yet, just across the border in Austria, 99.98 percent consent![7] The reason for this is not that people are more persuaded to consent in Austria, it's that they don't even have to decide. It's assumed. This is one of the classic examples of the default effect.

During our confinement, the household chores have definitely increased, as more people spend more time in the house, it creates more work. So, it's natural to want to share the load and it will make them happier! However, is it really worth the endless arguments with our kids and teens about domestic chores? The best way to approach this is to completely avoid having to persuade at all. Agree the distribution of work with the children once. Set the expectation of who will do what and when; make it automatic and avoid the argument.

Bertie Bott's jobs

Or make a game of it! Bertie Bott's Every Flavour Beans are crazy. Why would anyone want to eat sweets when there's a reasonable chance you might eat earwax or even vomit flavour? The reason is simple: it's fun (and it probably has something to do with intermittent reinforcement)! So how about creating a Bertie Bott's Every Flavour task jar? Fill it with a range of tasty tasks like 'Go and get a cookie' or 'Let's play Lego' through to 'Vacuum the living room' and 'Do the dishes'.

Workout together

We talked about exercise earlier, but increasingly research is showing the power of exercise for building togetherness. It shows that couples who exercise together are happier in their marriage,[8] and feel more in love.[10] So, if you don't already exercise with your partner, now might be a great time to start!

2. Rituals of togetherness

Research shows that rituals increase our enjoyment of experiences because they are predictable, and so help build our anticipation.[11] Rituals work on two principles: the activities are extremely specific and therefore build anticipation; there is a rhythm with which they happen, so they are more likely to happen. Activities become events when they are anticipated; and the events happen more often when they are habitual.

Date nights
I can't remember where I first heard the term but I'm a big fan of 'date nights'. This is the practice of putting a regular night aside, often once a week, for a nice, one-on-one meal with your partner. I'm told even Barack and Michelle have a date night. Dulcie and I have our own rules for date nights. Pre-confinement, these meals were four courses but now, we have trimmed them down to two. She cooks one and I cook the other. The covid twist is that the entire meal has to be cooked from what is already in the house. We're finding that the creativity (and weird combinations) that get produced add more energy than just following recipes. The anticipation, the creating and the cooking are every bit as part of the experience as the meal itself.

Family meals
The most important ritual for any family is eating together. Particularly through this crisis. For example, research shows that eating together (without TV or phones, of course) is strongly

linked to increased wellbeing and positivity,[12] more resilience,[13] and a greater sense of security and togetherness.[14] Yet US research over the last three decades shows a consistent reduction in the amount of time families spend preparing food and eating together.[15] My family always eats together, but often at our kitchen bar. We have intentionally started eating our evening meals in the dining room, to make them feel like more of an occasion. You could even expand on the idea of a date night and do a family version with each person cooking one course – let the chaos and connection (and cleaning up afterwards) begin!

Three cups of tea
Our most important ritual is our 'three cups of tea' mornings. Every Saturday and Sunday, we sit down for a tea drinking marathon. We cover more ground in those three teas, conversationally, than we might do in days otherwise. We digest what's going on in the news, how our kids (and we) are coping, plan our finances, we discuss the children and we dream. We are seldom more together than over those cups of tea. So, we stretch out the moment. We linger longer together.

3. Play together

Our brain is happiest when everything lines up: our goals, our thoughts and our attention. When we face a lot of novelty and uncertainty, we get knocked off course. Our thoughts become chaotic, hurried and splintered. This mental state is called *psychic entropy*;[16] it is unpleasant. At times of confusion, we need activities that help us to focus because that creates mental alignment and happiness. So how do we do this?

Mihaly Csikszentmihalyi, professor at Claremont Graduate University, wanted to understand happiness. Through years of research, one of the first things he found was that happiness is not lying on a beach sipping cocktails! He found that people's biggest highs, their peak moments, weren't relaxing or passive at all, but highly active. He described these times as *flow* experiences.[17] When we're in flow, we are deeply immersed in our chosen activity. Flow experiences are the very opposite of psychic entropy: our intentions, thoughts and actions are perfectly aligned; our consciousness is coherent and organised. We achieve happiness through deep engagement in what we are doing, whatever it is. We don't need to wait until this crisis is over to find happiness, we can start by deciding to focus, 100 percent, on what we're doing. To stretch every fibre of our being to improve or excel in that task or activity. The children's bath time, the monthly sales report or the washing up all offer opportunities for great happiness but only if we sink our attention into them with reckless abandon.

We are more likely to experience flow when we challenge ourselves, through goals and competition, and when the activity requires concentration. This is the power of family play. When we play together, whether it's Monopoly, charades or *War Thunder*, it forces us to focus and creates moments of shared flow. Psychic entropy is banished for a while, as we align in shared happiness.

Take a break, build a light saber

Play creates moments of flow and joy, but it can also help restore attention. We discussed breaks earlier. One of the most powerful ways to restore attention is to change your focus and energy; to play. Why not hire your children as play consultants? In your working week, their job is to help you play instead of taking a coffee break (sedentary caffeine stops have been associated with more fatigue.)[18] Instead, how about building a light saber, or making a den, or playing Twister!

You'll emerge re-energised and primed for focus and creativity, and they'll love it too.

BEING TOGETHER

Over the coming weeks and months of your confinement, it's not enough to 'spend time' with our loved ones. We also have to share attention. Too often, as MIT professor Sherry Turkle found in her book *Alone Together*, this time we spend with loved ones in the same location, is not really together at all. We're consumed in our own digital worlds and perforate any conversations we might have with grabs and glances at digital devices. Being together – truly being together – means sharing attention. Our current confinement is a great place to practise and relearn how to be together, unaided and uninterrupted by devices. That is where trust is built, and that is where joy comes from.

1. Bursting bubbles

Our technology is allowing us to connect from our confinement. Our children can stay connected with friends, we collaborate across the globe and teachers can still engage with pupils. While technology is helping us to connect to the world, it can also isolate us in our homes. As it allows us to connect to people far and wide, it sucks our presence away from those who are near. We wander around in a private bubble, physically present, but mentally elsewhere – and that's not good for our relationships with those who are near.

Here's the challenge. Burst through your bubbles. Through this confinement, double the amount of time you, and those you live with, are simultaneously out of your bubbles, together mentally, connected and sharing attention. For example, create screen-free time or build a cool phone amnesty box to put everyone's phones out of sight (research shows people like you less when you put a phone on the table during a conversation).

Practise the pause

In a famous experiment, social psychologists John Darley and Daniel Batson ran an experiment to show the effect of haste and helping. Trainee priests were going to give a lecture on The Good Samaritan (a parable about helping people) on the other side of town. Just before leaving for the lecture, some trainees were told they were running late, others that they had plenty of time. The effects were dramatic. Only 10 percent of the trainee priests who were late stopped to help a man who collapsed in front of them (who they had no way of knowing was an actor). Of those with more time, 63 percent stopped![19]

When we are in a rush, we are less likely to stop for other people. Our haste makes us more self-centred, stuck in our own bubble of importance. We are more likely to ignore or put other people on pause in our haste to do whatever we are in a rush to do.

Over this period, practise doing the reverse. As trivial as moments of connection may appear, pause. Ask yourself, is your desire to prioritise busyness over your loved one valid or is it just a result of your pace? Slow down for a moment to be present and together. You might find, as we have, that these pauses become the highlights of your day. One minute we may be tidying the kitchen, the next helping to attach a propeller to a Lego biplane, watching a lizard or dressing a doll. We'll be plunged into special moments of togetherness that are light and trivial, and in that triviality we'll smile and connect more.

2. Conversations

In the UK there has been a big TV campaign over the last year or so. It's called 'Get Britain Talking'. It involved programmes on ITV pausing, and the presenters explaining why talking matters, and giving the nation a minute to chat. It was initiated based on research showing that there had been a 48 percent increase in anxiety and depression in children since 2004.[20] The research showed the most powerful possible strategy to combat this is conversation in families.

The campaign proposes a number of conversation starters, to help us all get back into the habit of talking. These range from the weird and playful, to the sensible and serious:

- Would you rather be covered in fur or scales?
- Which movie character is most like you/me?
- How are you feeling today?
- What song do you listen to when you're angry?
- What have you been thinking about today?
- What questions do you have about coronavirus?

It doesn't much matter how you start, just that you do start, in curiosity and giving your full attention.

Be vulnerable
Another study of mental health in the UK found that while 82 percent of people feel more meaningful conversations at home would be beneficial for their mental health (particularly at a time like this); 46 percent keep their worries to themselves for fear of looking silly. None of us wants to appear weak, stupid or over-anxious. We might have concerns, and we might even have loved ones asking us how we are, but our willingness to open up is not based on the right question; it's based on something else.

As we go through this crisis, many of us will want to appear strong for our family. However, there can be an issue if you appear too strong. In *your* perfect positivity and strength, *my* anxiety can feel more like a weakness; even shameful.

If you want your loved ones to feel able to share their worries and weaknesses, we need to be willing to share ours first. If we are willing to be vulnerable, we allow others to believe their anxieties are natural, and feel safe to talk.

Family journal

I read about a family with a great covid ritual to trigger conversations: a family journal. Every day, each person would write something, draw something or cut out a picture that captured something important about the day for them. Each evening, the family would come together, explain what they'd come up with, and it would get glued into the page for that day. It is not only a chance to have great conversations, sharing how people are feeling; they are creating memories for the future, their own story of this historic time, together.

3. Savour together

Martin Seligman and his team[21] have developed a practice that will make you and your children happier. It's a simple activity, and it works better than Prozac! Here's how it goes. Every night, write down three things about the day that went well, or that you are happy about. Write a little bit of detail but you don't need to go overboard. That's it!

It works because, especially in times like this, we tend to over-focus on the negative; we ruminate and worry. This simple activity can help to rebalance our focus.

I've adapted it to work with my children. For years I would ask, on the drive home from school, "How was your day?" It was a boring question and I got perfunctory answers like "Good" (full stop). One day I asked instead, "What were the best three things today?" The conversation was infinitely richer; the children started thinking and vying with each other to come up with the best answers. It has become a regular and brilliant conversation for the children and me, and has helped to strengthen our relationship. I also like to think that, through this crisis, it might make a small impact on supporting their happiness.

Happy attacks

How good are you at savouring the moment? How good are you at lingering appreciatively in an experience, at plunging your full attention into the sensation or thought?

Here's a simple but sticky habit to use, to help you and those you are with savour a great moment of togetherness. It was created by Barry Horner, my father-in-law, an artist and an inspirational figure. At seemingly random moments – during dinner, a conversation or an activity – he will call out, "I'm having a happy attack!" He does this when he notices he is really enjoying that moment. This works on three levels: it helps him to savour great moments as they happen (how often do we realise times were great only after the moment has passed?), it invites others to savour the moment, and it is sticky – it easily becomes a habit.

Through your covid confinement, share your happy attacks and savour together!

Celebrate better

Shelly Gable, professor of psychology at the University of California, has demonstrated that how we celebrate is a better predictor of relationship strength than how we argue.[22] It appears that how we behave in those moments of triumph and joy makes a huge difference, it can either build or undermine the relationship.

So, what is the secret of a great celebration? Martin Seligman suggests that our responses are either passive, *simple statements*, or active, *asking questions*.

News: "The loaf of bread I've just baked has risen perfectly."

Passive celebration: "That's great news. Well done."

Active celebration: "That's amazing. What did you do differently? When did you first realise it was going to rise so well? How does it smell?"

It isn't hard to see which is better. Yet after I came across this distinction, I became painfully aware how often I reverted to passive celebrations with my children. The news of an A in English would get a brief, "Brilliant. I'm so proud of you." My responses were heartfelt and true, and they were well received, but they were unsubstantial.

I now celebrate better. Real celebration isn't about verbal pats on the back and drive-by congratulations. It's about taking the time to help the other person – partner, child or friend – to celebrate. It's about urging them to relive the experience and joining them in their emotions.

As moments for celebration occur over this period, don't congratulate; ask, relive and savour. Your celebration will bring you closer together.

CONNECTING TOGETHER

Thank goodness for Facebook, Whatsapp and Instagram!

Those of you who know my work may be surprised to hear me say this. But our ability as a society to reach out and connect with others beyond the confines of our building has made our isolation more social. Yet we also know that these amazing tools also pose a challenge. In a study of over 5,000 adults, increases in Facebook usage lead to reductions in self-reported physical health, mental health and life satisfaction.[23] So how do we still stay connected with those beyond our walls in a way that will improve our confinement?

1. Less is more

Tim Kasser, psychologist at Knox College, has done some amazing research into values. In particular he explored the difference between *affinity* and *popularity*. Affinity means being together and deepening key relationships. This stands in contrast to the attempt to be popular across the larger population. I had always lumped all kinds of socialising together, regarding intimacy with close friends and family as the same thing, albeit on a different scale, to banter and friendliness at a party. His research made me question this.

Kasser's research relates to people's priorities. Are they aspiring to have deeper relationships with close friends and family or to become more popular and have more friends? His findings indicate that those with a powerful focus on affinity tend to enjoy happiness, health and mental wellbeing. On the other hand, the reverse was found with those who strove for popularity: they were less happy, more depressed and more anxious. It seems that striving to deepen and strengthen important relationships is nourishing, fulfilling and life-enhancing. Going endlessly for 'more' friends is a great way to have a miserable life.

So, when it comes to our use of social media, the difference between these tools being positive sources of wellbeing or causes of depression appears to stem from the goals we are pursuing: closer connection with those few we truly love or popularity across many. In other words, even when it comes to relationships and social media, less is more.

Who are your fifteen?
The anthropologist Robin Dunbar showed there is a strong correlation between primate brain size and average group size.[24] It appears that when groupings of apes and monkeys get too big, they start to fall apart: they are too difficult to maintain. On the

basis of his work with other primates, Dunbar calculated the size of social groupings that humans could manage based on our cognitive capacity. His answer was 150. This has become known as 'Dunbar's number'. He then went a step further and started analysing historical records to see if social groupings, across cultures, tended to conform to his theory. He found remarkable consistency in the shape of social structures. He identified that our level of relationships can be thought of as concentric circles. We tend to have five people who are closest to us, who will often be immediate family and our partner (and in the house with us during the confinement). The next circle contains fifteen people, the next fifty, then 150. If you combine Dunbar's findings with those of Tim Kasser, the implication for me is that wellbeing, satisfaction and joy come from your fifteen. It is these magic fifteen people – your closest friends and family – who will trigger more flow experiences and happy attacks, and who will reduce your depression. The juice of life isn't in the 500 Facebook friends, it's in the fifteen.

If you remember nothing else from this chapter, remember this: over-invest your time and attention over your corona confinement in your fifteen. Spend time with them on Skype, keep connected with them on WhatsApp, and support them where you can. Any increase in the frequency and quality of these interactions will be a direct increase in the satisfaction you get from your confinement.

So, if those sharing your four walls are in your fifteen, who else is in your fifteen? What can you do to connect with them more and better?

2. Your Corona Support Team

While we are connected to more people, the number of close friends we can confide in seems to be dropping. One well-publicised study found social isolation in US adults had increased. For example, over two decades the average number of close confidants had dropped from three to two. The number of people who had no confidants at all had tripled. Finally, the percentage of people who only felt able to confide in family members has nearly doubled.[25]

One thing is clear. We will all need to confide and need social support over this period. We will probably also receive support from outside our home. People who are not part of the soap-opera of daily tribulations within your walls. People who you can vent with or get a fresh perspective from. People who will not judge you.

Take Mary, for example, a hardworking lawyer married to another lawyer. She loves Joe dearly, and he understands her well, but there are times she wants to howl with laughter and gossip. Joe doesn't do that for Mary, but Helen and Eva do. There are times Mary wants to create. She loves art and poetry, Joe doesn't, but Bill and Asiya do. At times she wants the unquestioning maternal love of her mum or to be with Lucy, her exercise and weight-loss partner.

For a moment, forget the people you care about most; think about who you need through this crisis. Who are your Corona Support Team?

Particularly, reflect on the following questions:

Emotional needs:
- Who just listens, without judgement, when I need to offload?
- Who helps you to see things positively?
- Who can you cry with?

Practical needs:
- Who gives great advice?
- Who is a brilliant teacher?
- Who knows stuff that's really useful right now?

Mood needs:
- Who makes you laugh or feel joyful?
- Who helps you 'take your mind of it all'?
- Who motivates you?

Two things will happen as you go through this. The first is that you will put some people's names in answer to a number of these questions. Great, they are part of your team! The second, is that you'll clarify other needs you have.

The simple point is that, with the best will in the world, your nearest and dearest will not be able to meet all of your needs. No one can. Instead of resenting that fact, reach out. Build your Corona Support Team.

3. Your community

Togetherness is everywhere these days. On a daily basis we hear of people like Andrea Pien, who offered $20 to those in need 'no questions asked'; people like Julia Lin, who is collecting food and distributing it to those who are struggling; or WhatsApp groups springing up on streets, turning strangers into neighbours. In our local town, Javea, one of the communities is arranging daily events, including bingo, carnivals (fancy-dress costumes are judged) and discos – all from their balconies!

In Robert Putnam's well-known book *Bowling Alone* he charted the decline of community. If there is any lesson to be drawn from this crisis, it is that we thrive in community with others – when we feel a sense of connection to groupings beyond our immediate families. I like to think that the start of this crisis marked the end of this decline, and from this day forward we will re-embrace the truth of our humanity: we are fundamentally social creatures.

So, in your confinement, reflect a while, and ask yourself, "What is your comminity?"

The un-talent show

A brilliant colleague of mine from Microsoft, Michele Skogerboe, has a fantastic way of maintaining her community through this crisis. She, and her husband David, have developed an 'un-talent show'. The idea is that everyone thinks of something they have always wanted to learn: a skill you want to improve or a project you want to get underway. They are invited to spend the quarantine period doing that thing. When the dust settles, and they're allowed to come together again, Michele and David will host the un-talent show. At that point, everyone can show off their 'thing', which must be something new – not something, in David's words, that people are 'already amazeballs' at.

This idea is to help create community and excitement, in anticipation of their moment of togetherness. It also encourages people to challenge themselves to learn, and in doing so build more flow into their confinement.

Giving More

When Matt Hancock, the UK's health secretary, asked for volunteers to help the 1.5 million vulnerable people in corona isolation, they hoped for 250,000 applicants. Within twenty-four hours, they already had twice that number of volunteers! These terrible times are triggering great displays of generosity around the world.

There's an old adage that it's better to give than receive. It turns out that this is supported by evidence. Research into altruism has persistently shown benefits to health, happiness and psycho-logical wellbeing. One study into sufferers of multiple sclerosis, for example, found that patients who offered support to other MS patients actually experienced more benefits than those they helped in terms of confidence, self-esteem, depression and daily functioning.[26] Another study showed that giving also builds our resilience, helping to protect us from the stress of modern life.

What could you give to others that would be meaningful?

Who would you like to help?

What do you want your corona contribution to be?

This might sound a crazy idea, given how much you have on at present. Yet, counter-intuitively, researchers have found that one of the best ways of feeling a sense of time-affluence (that you have lots of time) is to give it away! Those people that gave their time to others appeared to feel less rushed.[27]

Over the last few decades we have retreated into our gated communities, behind our fences and into our nuclear families. This, it would appear, is our moment to emerge. As the virus confines us behind our walls, this is our generation's opportunity to reverse the retreat from community. To reach out the hand of help to strangers, the needy and the unloved in the simple, but most human act of generosity.

SUMMARY FOR TOGETHER@HOME

Doing together

1. *Working together*
    Research shows that helping with chores makes teens hap-pier and more positive as they feel more connected to the family. Don't spend your time asking though, create default

expectations through this crisis: a jobs rota. Or make it playful with a Bertie Bott's Every Flavour task jar.

2.   *Rituals of togetherness*
     Rituals increase anticipation and stickiness. Create rituals of togetherness for family meals. How about 'three cups of tea' or a date night? Get imaginative. The more specific and unique to your family, the more effective they'll be.

3.   *Play together*
     When we challenge ourselves, we create flow experiences – moments of deep immersion and happiness. When we play together, we trigger collective flow. Use the power of play to refresh yourself, use breaks to switch from serious work to play: take a break, build a light saber!

Being together

1.   *Bursting bubbles*
     We might be in the same space with those we love but are we together in shared attention? Beware the digital bubbles we all inhabit. Build screen-free time into family life. Also, bubbles are also created by haste: practise the pause when your loved ones need you.

2.   *Conversations*
     There have been big increase in childhood anxiety and depression. So get talking! If you want to encourage your kids to open up, be vulnerable – talking about your worries makes them feel less silly about sharing theirs. Maybe create a family journal to chart your stories through this crisis.

3. *Savour together*

    Make happiness a shared activity by savouring together: call out "I'm having a happy attack!" Not only does this help you savour, it encourages moments of happy togetherness. Also, celebrate by asking questions rather than drive-by congratulations, going from "Well done" to "Tell me more!"

Connecting together

1. *Less is more*

    Trying to be popular will make you miserable; trying to get closer to the fifteen people who matter most to you will drive joy and health into your life. So who are your fifteen? More importantly, what will you do to stay connected through the crisis; to love and be loved?

2. *Your Corona Support Team*

    Also, however much we love our immediate family, our personality and our current needs are broader. Identify your Corona Support Team: people who meet your main covid confinement practical and emotional needs.

3. *Your community*

    Years of retreating away from community into our nuclear families is on the reverse. We see community being reborn around the world. Who is your community? How about creating events like the 'un-talent' show, or give more (generosity is good for your health and happiness).

WORK@HOME

This section addresses how to work at home. As we settle into our confinement we still have to deliver, both in our paid work and in our family demands. We'll explore how to commit to work that matters and to your colleagues when they and your manager can't see you; renegotiating work commitments as your family commitments change; and how to bring the full force of attention into your work in the midst of family, chaos and high emotion. Finally, we'll discuss how to use this crisis as a chance for work and career innovation. We'll do all this because, no matter how great your family time is through this crisis, if you can't make work, work, you're not going to thrive!

Chapter 5

Commit@Home

The picture showed the bruised face of a young woman. She is Alessia Bonari, an exhausted nurse from Milan. She explained that the bruises had come from wearing ill-fitting protective equipment nine hours a day. "I am physically tired because the protective devices are bad, the lab coat makes me sweat and once dressed I can no longer go to the bathroom or drink for six hours … I am psychologically tired, as are my colleagues, who have been in the same condition for weeks … I'm afraid to go to work … because the mask may not adhere to my face, or I may have accidentally touched myself with dirty gloves." Bonari didn't share her picture on Instagram to moan, she had a purpose. She goes on to ask of those reading her post "not to frustrate the efforts we are making … stay at home … I can't afford the luxury of going back to my quarantined house. I have to go to work and do my part. You do yours, I ask you please."

Bonari is one of millions of healthcare workers around the world on the frontline, putting themselves in harm's way to save the rest of us. They face infection with painful protection – or none at all – and open up their families to risk every day, as they care for those struggling to survive covid-19. The spontaneous

applause from balconies is a small sign of the respect and grati-
tude we all feel worldwide.

However, it is not our applause that keeps Bonari and her
global community of colleagues going. It is her commitment. As
she explains, these challenges, risks and discomforts "won't prevent us from doing our job as we've always done. I will continue
to take care of my patients because I am proud and I love my job."

Our challenges may be different to those on the frontline, but
we have them nonetheless. This chapter is about committing to
what matters at work while working from home; committing to
colleagues and to collaboration, as you work in isolation; and to
the challenges of supporting your family through this crisis. Like
Bonari, these commitments are grounded in pride and love.

COMMIT TO WHAT MATTERS

When it comes to committing at work, I am talking about procrastination. It is one thing to identify your Covid Compass and your
Big 3, it is quite another thing to convert that to persistent action
in a full family home. Let's not forget, this period is tough, and
procrastination is a natural response to overwhelm.

This section offers practical suggestions on how to get started
from the comfort and emotions of your home, out of sight of your
manager. However, there is another element to procrastination.
We often put off the hard, impactful work because the easy reactivity of email and microtasks asks less of us, it is less stressful.[1]
This is likely to be especially true these days, when our ambient
anxiety levels are high. So rather than work on that big project,
we might feel compelled to flop into email, fold the laundry or
knock off a few tasks from our list. However, busy activity is no
way to thrive, it's just a form of procrastination.

1. Inertia

> *[Inertia] is a power of resisting by which every*
> *body ... endeavours to preserve its present*
> *state ... of rest.*
>
> Sir Isaac Newton

Using momentum

One of the best ways to overcome inertia-based procrastination is to use your current momentum. For example, when hotel maids were told how much exercise they were already doing in their daily job, they started exercising more![2] In chapter 2 we discussed routines and anchor habits. What's critical here is that your starting work habits are connected to your early morning habits, so you use their momentum. For example, on a typical work day, we have breakfast together as a family in the kitchen. Then Dulcie and I have a cup of tea on our own. Then I shower, dress and start work. At no point in this series of events do I need to decide 'should I start work?', it is an automatic pattern of habitual behaviour. The momentum of my morning means there is no inertia.

Peer pressure

Your work patterns in normal life are propelled by a sense of what 'on time' and 'late' mean at your work. Even if our work does not have formal start times, there are usually unwritten expectations. These are reinforced more by peer pressure than any formal process.

Without peer pressure, and without a start time for your work, it means you have to overcome inertia every day. So, agree as a family what on time and late means. Start work at the same time, together, and allow peer pressure to defeat inertia.

Start on big tasks

Marla Cilley is a selfhelp guru focused on housekeeping. Many of her clients get overwhelmed into inertia by the scale of the mess in their homes. She developed a policy of the 'five minute room rescue' whereby you enter the dirtiest, messiest room in the house bringing with you a kitchen timer. You tidy and clean with fury, but only for five minutes –then you stop. At that point, people feel motivated by the progress they have made. They are already in motion, so they keep going.[3]

This works for getting started on the big, important but scary tasks. Commit to a twenty-minute burst of activity. Set your timer and start. If you are really struggling to motivate yourself, plan a reward for when you complete your twenty minutes. Once you've started, momentum will do the rest.

2. How to get in the mood

A very common cause of procrastination is not being 'in the mood'. This is particularly true of the big things. So, in these volatile times, where emotions are a little less stable than usual, how do you help yourself get in the right mood more often for your important work?

Get the chemicals right

Amy Arnsten discovered that the degree to which the prefrontal cortex is operating effectively depends upon the right balance of two chemicals: dopamine and norepinephrine.[4] Over the coming months, you might not just have to manage your mood but the working moods of your children too. Here's how to do it.

Too little dopamine: You will feel bored and lethargic. Use reversal theory. Shift the goal of the task to having fun or being creative, and turn on some music!

Too much dopamine: You will feel scattered and distracted. Switch off or minimise your digital distractions. If you're trying to do two things at once, stop! Move to the quietest place of your home.

Not enough norepinephrine: You will feel a lack of urgency. Put the pressure on. Arrange a review meeting to discuss your progress tomorrow!

Too much norepinephrine: You will feel 'Ahhhhh, it's too much!' Reduce your stress and anxiety by breaking the task into small chunks. Focus on what is in your control. Remind yourself that you can only do your best. That is enough!

If you have children at home, all of the above can also apply to supporting your children in their schoolwork.

3. Dependence

The final cause of procrastination is dependence. This is dominated by the word *when*: "I'll do it *when* I've tidied the house", "I'll do it *when* I've read all my emails", "I'll do it *when* I have got the children settled."

When has become a very big word in our house! It's one thing to leave the breakfast chaos as you leave for work. It's another thing to stare at it all day, and even worry if your colleagues will see it on your conference calls! If your coming months are dominated by *when*, you might find you never quite get round to your Covid Compass. *When* is always well-intentioned but it is also toxic.

When is a sequence thing: you feel you shouldn't do your tax return until you've first done the email or the dishes, or you won't relax. As we know, of course, by the time you've emptied your inbox (and then the sink) there often isn't time to do the tax return. So instead, start with the most important tasks (your Big

3) or the ones that will bring most joy to you and your family. If you catch yourself saying *when* too often, try changing it to *then*. Flip the sequence. Instead of "I'll paint *when* I've got on top of the house" change it to "I'll paint *then* I'll get on top of the house." A single letter change could change your life!

COMMIT TO COLLABORATION

Over the last decade, the amount of time we all spend collabrating has increased by more than 50 percent.[5] Some of this, of course, is about the incessant emails and mind-numbing meetings. Some of it also represents a real shift in the way work is done. Work is getting more complex, and our technology more advanced. We increasingly rely on the expertise of others, in our teams and across our businesses, to enable us to do our job. The unit of work is shifting from the individual to the team.

This section explores how to commit to our colleagues during our confinement. How to collaborate and connect virtually in order to perform, innovate and learn together but also in a way that deepens those relationships. I write this based not just on research but also on my personal experience. Every single one of my colleagues lives in a different country, and often in a different time zone. I have had to learn to deliver impactful work collaboratively from a distance but also how to build trust and friendship.

1. Social distance and virtual distance

We are all immersed in social distancing right now, keeping space between us in order to prevent the spread of the virus. Psychologically speaking, we tend to make a connection between distance and the strength of our connections to others.[6] We even refer to people, for example, as being 'close to us', using spatial language to describe social feelings. What might be the effect on our teams and collaboration as we work at a distance from our colleagues?

Karen Sobel Lojeski, an expert in navigating the virtual workplace, has done a lot of research into this very question.[7] She has identified an emotional detachment that often happens when teams connect digitally and work from separate locations. She calls this *virtual distance*; and it can have quite an impact. Across 800 teams, and many industries, she found those with high virtual distance had significantly lower levels of innovation, trust, engagement, satisfaction, learning and performance.[8] It is important to stress, virtual distance is not an automatic result of distributed teams. It's just there are specific factors, unique to the context of teams who work virtually, that we have to address if we want to avoid it.

Operational factors come from the practical challenges of connecting over digital media. Digital communication is often more task-focused than face-to-face conversations, with less small talk, so the likelihood of confusion and misunderstandings multiplies. When communicating electronically, we don't automatically have the same shared context. We don't know what is happening for that person at that moment; we find it hard to adjust our communication to adjust to their context and build understanding.

The *affinity* factor is the degree of inter-connectedness we feel towards others in the team. In China they have a term 'guanxi' (pronounced GWAN-shee), which means successful work happens when we start with the relationship. This connection is important to all teams; it's just we need to be even more intentional about doing this virtually.

Lojeski's research shows that a lack of affinity is the biggest cause of virtual distance, followed by operational factors. In fact, a lack of affinity had twice the impact on virtual distance than geographical separation.[9] So physical distance is not necessarily a problem, nor is connecting virtually. We just need to be more intentional about building human connections and shared understanding.

2. Building virtual connection

Collaborating effectively in virtual teams requires intentionality. Some of the relationship building interactions that would occur by default when people work alongside each other need to be intentionally inserted into virtual conversations. Here are some thoughts on how to do this over the coming weeks.

Virtual tours

Delivering Happiness is a completely distributed business. All its employees work virtually, so they have had to learn ways to make it work. For example, they ask newly formed teams, or new team members, to give video tours of their workspaces. This allows colleagues to form mental images of one another and where they are working from.

One of the positive things that has happened as we've entered confinement, is that we've been invited into the homes of our long-time colleagues. We see their working location, pictures on their wall, children walking by in the background. Taking a moment to do a virtual introduction to your home context can build a human connection.

Schedule breaks at the virtual water cooler

This is a group version of a virtual coffee. Remember, Bank of America experienced a $15 million rise in profits when they scheduled breaks, to encourage more small talk. Small talk is the secret sauce behind a lot of collaboration: it is the social glue that bonds a team, it helps keep others up-to-date with everyone's lives and therefore connected.

Schedule coffee breaks or a lunch break with your colleagues. Arrange a video call, and come with your water, coffee or food. You're not talking business, this is social; but then, social is good business.

Building shared context

In psychological terms, we start every conversation with a 'same as me' bias. The assumption that another's worldview, their understanding and motivation will be the same as ours. As we engage in the complex dance of face-to-face conversation, we read and respond to the signals we see. These help us to move beyond our 'same as me' starting point. Often, in electronic communication, there is nothing to challenge our bias, and so we plough on, ignorant of the gulf in understanding or alignment.

Francesca Gino's research shows that the best way to minimise bias and misunderstanding is through kindling curiosity. It also increases innovation. Ask people their view and get them to expand, and listen carefully. Since there is less to see in a virtual context, we must intentionally increase what we hear to compensate.

3. Virtual meeting tips

So let's get practical. How do you increase the effectiveness of your virtual meetings?

Watch your background

Our children are having their lessons via Zoom through this crisis. At the end of the first week, we had a complaint from Ben and Seren. They both sleep on the top bunk in their bedrooms.

They also have thick mattresses. So, in both cases, their mattress is higher than the safety rail at the side of their bed. No problem, we thought, we'll just use the safety bed guard they had used as toddlers. It was only towards the end of that first week when they both had classmates ask why they had bed guards on their beds. Not cool! Check your background before going on a call.

Is anyone listening?

This is always a great thing to wonder. Research by Intercall showed that 65 percent of people are doing other work when in a conference call, 55 percent are eating or making food, 25 percent are playing video games and 9 percent are exercising.[10] 27 percent of people even admitted to having fallen asleep during a call! It's not to say that our attention is perfect in normal meetings but this is another level! At the very least, use your video. Not only does it increase a sense of connection, it increases attention. For example, one study found when video is used, the attention span of UK callers increased by 50 percent.

Dual channel the meeting

In-person meetings allow us to simultaneously pick up signals from everyone in the room, even when people are not speaking. It can be fairly easy to signal you want to speak, even while someone else is talking. This is less easy virtually. Actively use the chat box to allow others to contribute, in addition to the current speaker. How about using a 'hand raised' emoji in chat or agree in the team how you will signal "I want to speak."

Make it interactive

I had to put all this into practice recently. On a major culture project with Microsoft, a three-day in-person design session with key people from across the business was cancelled because of the crisis. However, Microsoft is committed to their culture, so we decided to do it virtually. We faced three big challenges: how do you make a three-day virtual session engaging and useful? How to run this effectively, given we had five facilitators, spread across three countries? Finally, we were using a virtual collaboration tool, Klaxoon, that none of us had ever used before.

In the end, the session was one of the best events I've ever been part of. So, what did we do and learn?

- Klaxoon works in Microsoft Teams. It allows everyone to submit ideas on virtual post-its. The group can then move and cluster them, and vote on them from anywhere in the world. It transformed the interactivity and engagement of the session. Even if you don't have a tool like Klaxoon, there are other options. For example, have everyone open a shared document in Microsoft O365, Google Docs or Slack. You can then collaborate on the document in real time.
- The five of us facilitators, Fred Lee, Michele Skogerboe, Craig DeWald, Laurie Asava and myself, established our roles clearly. We also set up a separate Teams chat group for our off-line, real-time conversations to align, review and plan. The effect felt like seamless collaboration for the participants.
- We found we had to get much clearer, in advance, of the activities we would do, and the outcomes we were trying to drive. This was forced on us by the virtual context; but also lead to better results.
- Human touches, done regularly, helped. Such as Fred's 'theme tunes'. He had everyone identify their theme tune as a warm-up exercise on day three. Throughout the day, he would play these songs at key moments!
- Finally, it felt to us that the session was more diverse and inclusive. Voices that we wouldn't normally expect to be heard in that group came through with clarity. It appeared the space created by being online, and also the habit of

starting with individual reflections on post-its, meant that all voices were heard.

As I mentioned before, great collaboration is completely possible virtually; it just needs a little more attention, imagination and human touches.

NEGOTIATE

In addition to committing to your big stuff and to your colleagues, there is a final aspect of commitment I want to explore. I don't imagine there is anyone who has moved into confinement, whose demands have not changed. True, you might not have your daily commute anymore but you also have additional educational and childcare duties, you might also have scheduling challenges due to your shared workspace. Whatever your challenges, your change in commitments can become a major source of stress unless you discuss them and renegotiate with your work and family.

1. Negotiate with yourself first

Rather than negotiate, we try and cope. We look at all our demands over this period and think "It's a lot but, I'll manage." Really what we're saying to ourselves is "I might not be able to manage but I certainly don't want to have that conversation with my manager!"

However, we're terrible at predicting how long things will take. Most of us under-estimate it by 50 percent![11] This is known as the *planning fallacy*. So, if you're thinking "I'll probably manage," I'm here to tell you that you're probably wrong and you should talk to your manager. Also remember, your manager is going through this crisis too. The last thing they want is for you to have problems because you didn't speak with them. They don't need you to be another problem on their list!

"Yes" is more likely than you think

Few of us relish negotiating about work. In fact, a lot of us actively avoid ever having these conversations. Part of the reason we do this is because we are sure the other person will say no. We assume negotiations will be painful and pointless.

In an interesting series of experiments at Cornell University, Francis Flynn and Vanessa Bohns gave people a challenge. They had to go up to a stranger and make a request. For example, "Can I use your phone?" Before making this request, everyone had to estimate how likely it was that the other person would say yes. People underestimated the likelihood of the other person agreeing by 50 percent! The reason for this is simple. The discomfort we feel about making this request makes us completely ignore the discomfort the other person would feel in saying no.

I was on a call with managers from around the world recently. They told me how this crisis had rekindled their passion for management. As we stumble through the crisis, these managers felt a desire to support their people in a way far beyond how they feel in normal times. Committing to help their team felt like a contribution they could make to society. It gave them a sense of purpose. Don't under-estimate the desire your manager will have to support you through covid. Your request to renegotiate might just give them a chance to show they care; a chance for them, in the heart of this crisis, to do something to help.

The positive "no"

For those of us who have tried to keep work and life separate, it might feel uncomfortable, even disloyal, to negotiate because of our personal life. For example, how do you negotiate your way out of a project because your daughter is struggling with her physics schoolwork?

Curiously, according to negotiation expert William Ury, the starting point for saying "No", is saying "Yes". Cancelling a commitment can feel like a negative act. You need to remind yourself you are doing it for an entirely positive reason: your daughter. In other words, you are saying no to the project because you are saying a big yes to your daughter. Getting really clear on your big yes makes saying no a whole lot more motivational.

2. Negotiations with work

Don't haggle!
When we think of negotiation, we think of haggling. We start low, and they start high; then we argue furiously to try to change each other's prices. Roger Fisher and William Ury, founders of the Harvard Negotiation Project, don't think that's the best way. What Fisher and Ury suggest is that we focus on discussing our needs instead. Once you both agree on each other's needs, you are no longer competing. You are working together to find solutions to needs you both agree with.

Let's imagine you want to negotiate about your conference calls. Since the lockdown, there are four of you working from home. Your son and daughter have Zoom lessons all morning, and they need silence to participate. Since all available rooms are being used, you decide you will negotiate call-free mornings. You explain what your situation is, and your need to let your children have quiet in order to study. You then explore your manager's needs. She agrees that while you can excuse yourself from some of the meetings, she needs you to attend one of the daily morning meetings. Now you know each other's needs, you can collaborate on a solution together. This might be moving the important meeting to the afternoon, or joining the call on mute, making any contributions via chat.

I find when negotiating about lifestyle issues, focusing on underlying needs is much more useful. When we talk about our real needs, it's powerful and authentic. More than that, it leaves both people feeling good.

Don't argue

It's also not smart to argue! This is because of something called *cognitive dissonance*: when we argue for something, we increase our belief that we are right. In other words, the very act of arguing drives both people in the negotiation apart!

Let's say you want to spend quality time with your family in this stressful period. You could storm onto a call and ask for a finishing time of 4:30 p.m. This might work but it could easily lead to an argument. On the other hand, if the conversation is framed in terms of needs, you can build on agreements. "My work and my family are both important to me ... [agree] ... I want to find the right balance in this difficult time ... [agree] ... Will you help me find a solution that works for you and me? ... [agree] ...". If your manager disagrees with anything, don't argue, ask them to expand. Try and understand their needs. This will then help you to refocus the conversation on agreements.

Because

There is a magic to the word 'because'. Research by Ellen Langer, professor of psychology at Harvard University, found that simply using the word 'because' in a request increases the likelihood that you will get what you want by half.[12] Whether you are saying no to a request, or asking permission to delay a deadline, if you include 'because', your argument will be seen as more rational and acceptable.

Linking back to the earlier example, "I want to step off this project *because* my daughter is struggling with her physics, *because* her education is important to me and *because*, while her school is closed, I am the only one who will be able to help her."

3. Difficult conversations at home

Over the coming months of claustrophobic confinement, where everyone's work is a distraction to everyone else, family routines are disrupted and personal space is invaded, tensions and arguments will arise. To make this into a positive period, we also have to be willing and able to address these tensions in a useful manner.

One of the most useful books on difficult conversations I've ever read is from the Harvard Negotiation Project (clever folks). Without going through their whole philosophy and approach, I want to share three basic rules that really help, and they all have one thing in common. They are not about winning, they are more about understanding. They aim to create a learning conversation, so the conflict becomes an opportunity to grow your relationship.

I'm not arguing, I'm explaining why I'm right!

Jack, our eldest son, is an engineer in heart and in personality. He was even bought a t-shirt that reads 'Engineer: I'm not arguing, I'm explaining why I'm right!'. It's appropriate for him, and a great reminder for all of us.

The first thing we should all attempt to avoid in our families are the arguments focused on proving we are right. When we argue with loved ones about something that happened, both sides think they are right. As I mentioned above, the more we argue about what happened, the more we each convince ourselves that we are right and they are wrong. This isn't surprising because we both have different information and we have a different set of personal interests.

The point is, the longer you argue about who is right, the further you are from a resolution. So, stop arguing! Don't *X-Files* your way to resentment ('The truth is out there!'). Move from focusing on proving truth (or that you're right), to trying to understand their perspectives. How do they see things?

A practical thing that can help is the 'and stance'. Rather than thinking either you are right *or* they are right, think of your view as valid *and* theirs is too. It is simultaneously valid that you prepared the dinner with love *and* they don't like it; that they were making too much noise *and* you over-reacted; that you've given up a lot of your time to teach them maths *and* they are not enjoying the lesson because you make them feel stupid.

Don't assume they meant it!

We often get embroiled in conversations about intentions. This isn't helpful for two reasons. We are often wrong when judging other people's intentions, and we are nearly always ungenerous. Secondly, when it comes to ourselves, we don't judge ourselves by our actions as much as by our intentions. However, even good intentions don't justify bad outcomes. Instead, keep the conversation focused on impact: "When you said that, the impact on me was . . ."

Don't play the blame game!

Finally, don't play the blame game. In your head it's pretty clear, they are to blame, and they should apologise! The problem is, that's your story and their story is different. If you are trying to guide a conversation towards them accepting blame, you're onto a no-win scenario. Either you force them into accepting blame, in which case they resent you for it. Or they don't accept blame, and you resent them. The simple fact is, in most cases, both of you had a part to play. Talk instead about how you both contributed. It moves the conversation away from judgement and towards learning. So, if your child is screaming at you because their iPad isn't charged up for their school lessons, don't scream "It's not my fault! It's your iPad!" Try focusing instead on understanding your role in the issue, in their view. Only then might they be willing to listen to your view on their need to take personal responsibility!

SUMMARY FOR COMMIT@HOME

Commit to what matters

1. *Inertia*
   Procrastination is often about inertia. So, don't start; continue! Anything you can do to build off the momentum of your daily rhythms will help deal with inertia. Or use peer pressure: create family start and stop times for work. Finally, if it's a big, scary task, start small: just for 20 minutes!

2. *How to get in the mood*
   Get in the mood by managing your chemicals. Dopamine: too little, and you feel lethargic, too much and you'll be scattered. Norepinephrine: too little means no urgency, too much and you'll be stressed. Take simple steps to increase or decrease the dopamine buzz and the norepinephrine pressure.

3. *Dependence*
   When in lockdown with your family and all the household mess, it's easy to get stuck saying "I'll do that report *when* I've tidied away the breakfast." Change *when* to *then*. "I'll do that report *then* I'll . . ." That single change of a letter can change everything!

Commit to collaboration

1. *Virtual distance*

   When we are physically distant from our colleagues and teams, virtual distance can develop which reduces innovation, satisfaction and performance. The biggest causes are not distance or digital, it's human connection and shared context. Intentionally build human connection into meetings.

2. *Building virtual connection*

   How about building connection by encouraging people to give virtual tours of their workspace at home. Or synchronise breaks and have virtual team coffee breaks. Be mindful of building shared context, you might need to start with more background information.

3. *Virtual meeting tips*

   Watch your background – there's only so much you want your colleagues to see! Remember, virtual meetings don't require as much attention, so make conversations and meetings interactive. Use chat so people can contribute even when they are not speaking.

Negotiate your commitments

1. *Negotiate with yourself first*

   The first conversation to have is with yourself! "Yes" is 50 percent more likely than you think … so, ask! Remind yourself of your big yes: what have you chosen to say yes to, which is leading to this conversation. Connecting to values can remind us that saying no is not a negative act!

2. *Negotiations with work*
    Too often we think of negotiation as a haggle. Instead, focus
    on your underlying needs, and understand theirs; then find
    a creative solution together. Try not to argue, it drives you
    both further from agreement. Don't forget the power of
    explaining your 'because'.

3. *Difficult conversations*
    Three things not to do during our difficult family covid
    conversations: don't try to prove that you are right (and they
    are wrong), take the 'and stance' instead; don't assume you
    understand their intentions (you don't and you'll be ungen-
    erous!); finally, don't get into the blame game.

Chapter 6

Think@Home

Anne Sikken is trying to work at home. She is a digital media consultant. She is also the wife of an overtime-working anaesthesiologist and mother of two sons under ten. One thing she rapidly realised after the schools closed down in The Netherlands, was that her boys had different definitions of urgent and important than she had. For example, for them, the questions "Mama, do you have a towel to make a superhero cape?" or "Can we use the poop scoop to bury a dead mouse?" are so pressing that Mama needs to be interrupted. In fact, in one sixty-minute conference call, compelled by similarly pressing issues, they interrupted her thirty times!

As Lobke Vlaming, director of Parents & Education, a Dutch organisation which represents the interests of parents with school-based children, says "The separation of work, education and school is there for a reason. It's not an ideal combination when it all comes together at home."

For my own part, I was wondering how I'd start this chapter. Then, just as I was about to start writing about attention and focus, our son Ben started his drumming lesson via Zoom! In normal times, I might have paused my writing until I could hear myself think ... but these are not normal times.

This chapter is about how to think in a context of too much noise and distraction. It is about how to bring the full force of our intellect to bear on the projects, the conversations or the algebra that matters; and to do this despite superhero capes, dead mice and drums.

Three networks of attention

Michael Posner is a professor, cognitive neuropsychologist, and one of the leading experts on attention. He describes the three networks of attention as the *orienting*, the *alerting* and the *executive*. The orienting network is about direction. Neuroscientist Amishi Jha describes it as the 'flashlight of the mind'. The alerting network deals with depth or intensity of concentration. Finally, the executive is the boss. It determines how long attention lingers on any one topic. To think effectively means managing the direction, depth and duration of your attention. In the rest of this chapter I'll explain how to do this in these unprecedented times.

DIRECTION

We've probably all had those days when you start your morning full of great intentions. You work hard all day but as you finish work, you can't really remember what you accomplished! Managing your attention's direction is about addressing this experience. It's a set of habits that persistently direct your attention back onto what really matters, whether that's paid work or family time.

1. Pre-commit

How often do you make good decisions when you go to the supermarket really, really hungry? This is an example of *hot* and *cold* decision-making. When we're hungry, we're in the hot state: powerfully and immediately tempted by what we see. When we're not hungry, in the cold rational state, we choose quinoa salad! As economist George Loewenstein explains, "It's really easy to agree to diet when you're not hungry."

The same is true of work. We know from research that, given the choice between easy but dull, and interesting but hard, in the moment, people nearly always choose easy but dull. The problem is, those important things that you know you *should* focus on are usually interesting but hard. So, as you sit there with your first coffee, in that moment it's just more tempting to start with some easy stuff. So, you open your email.

Apply that in the context of a family-full apartment, unwashed dishes and a dog that needs walking, and the trouble gets multiplied. Our homes are hot zones full of activities that are tempting or just plain easy.

Eating frogs
One simple way to direct our attention to the stuff that matters comes from Brian Tracy's *Eat that Frog!*. The concept is that if you eat a frog first thing in the morning, anything else you do that day won't be too bad! Essentially Tracy is suggesting that, before you open your inbox or wash the breakfast dishes, set aside a slice of time to work on the biggest, scariest, most important project you are facing at that time; by confronting the task head on, everything else you need to do that day will seem easy.

This is an example of a pre-commitment. Studies show that when we commit to something in advance (when we're in a cold state) we are more likely to follow through with the action (in a hot state).[1] Here's how to apply this principle during the covid crisis:

- Decide today what 'frog' you want to eat first tomorrow (this might be a paid job or family chores).
- Decide when you will start, and how long you'll work on your 'frog'.
- Decide what you won't do before starting your frog (email, laundry, etc,)

2. What will I do next?

From the perspective of directing your attention, your effectiveness can be understood by what you do in a number of key transitions. I call these 'What will I do next?' (WWIDN) moments. As we finish a task, meeting, break or conversation we ask ourselves WWIDN. Each one of those moments is prone to hot decision-making; and each one of those moments sets you on a path of activity until your next transition.

The question is, what do you look at first? In most offices, the go-to places in WWIDN moments are the inbox and the to-do list; and neither place is very helpful. Let me be clear of my view on to-do lists. They are great places to dump tasks, to clear your 'monkey mind', as organisational expert David Allen would call it. However, they are not great as primary drivers of activity. The things we capture on to-do lists are the things that we are worried about forgetting, and so by definition, not that important.

So where should you go first as you are deciding WWIDN? The answer is simple: to your Big 3. Remember, your Big 3 might include paid work and family-focused items. Also remember, just because you go first to your Big 3, doesn't mean you never go into your inbox or to-do list. It's just you don't use them to decide how you prioritise: you already did that, and it's called your Big 3. The fact is, by starting with your Big 3, you are making sure you insert the opportunity cost of the tempting, busy activity into your decision-making process. You insert what really matters into your WWIDN moments.

3. Review your progress

Jerry Seinfeld, the comedian, was once asked why he was so funny. He explained it was because of a big calendar on his wall. He realised the best way to be funny was to write new material. Every day he spends writing new material, he draws a big, red cross on that date. He explained that, after time, the crosses formed chains, and that he didn't want to break the chain. Seinfeld has found a really simple way to monitor progress against what matters.

The thing is, attention is attracted to what is easy to monitor. When we move from seventy-seven emails to twenty-three we feel a sense of progress. The same is true when we go from eleven to-do list items to two. Yet it is harder to sense progress on the things that might appear on our Covid Compass: learning French, helping inspire children around mathematics or trying to identify innovative new go-to-market strategies. These are all harder to track but potentially more important.

Harvard Business School professor Teresa Amabile found that a sense of making progress on the work that really matters to us was perhaps our biggest motivator. She called this the *progress principle*.[2] To build this sense, spend time at the end of each day reviewing progress against your Big 3. Not only will this help you to redirect attention onto what matters, it will build your motivation through this period.

DEPTH

Depth is about your ability to concentrate and immerse yourself in an activity. Any of us might sit, free from distractions yet that doesn't guarantee deep immersion. By the same token, just because there is a lot of noise around you, does not mean you can't focus: think of how well you have worked in Starbucks. Here's a few ideas to help.

1. One thing at a time

Have you ever noticed that if you are walking while talking on your mobile phone and someone asks you a tough question, you stop moving while you think? You stop because you intuitively want to divert all your paltry mental resources to your prefrontal cortex.

Harold Pashler, distinguished professor of psychology at the University of California, has shown that we are not good at doing two things at once.[3] The reason for this is *dual-task interference*: our brains are not designed to multitask. Multitasking can drop the performance of a Harvard MBA student to that of an eight-yearold.[4] The only way to work around this is to focus on one thing at a time.

Closing files

Do you have those days when you have back-to-back conference calls, interrupted periodically with blasts of teaching and tidying? We know, as you go from call to call, you become less intelligent! This is because of attention residue: part of your attention is left processing the previous meeting, leaving you less attention to focus on your new call, or your kid's geography class.

This is a consequence of the Zeigarnik effect: the brain works on 'open' and 'closed' files. As we go from meeting to meeting, or task to task, files are opened. As long as these are opened, your processing power drops (and you get more tired). The critical thing that determines whether a file stays open, is whether the task or project at hand is finished. For example, most calls we attend are about on-going projects, and as such, seldom finished.

To improve your focus and thinking power, you can develop a very simple habit. Close your files. This is exactly the same technique we used to reduce churning in chapter 1. At the end of a meeting or unfinished activity, spend a moment writing a plan, or the very next steps you'll take to progress this and when you'll do it. That helps to close your files and allows you to focus on your next call.

Don't pollute your brain

Imagine you are helping your child study. They go to the toilet, so you think 'I'll just check my email'. You have just polluted your brain. We've glanced at our messages, even though we know we won't be able to properly respond now because we can hear the toilet flush. We do these micro-glances almost reflexively whenever we have a moment alone. Yet they do nothing more than reduce how present we are in that moment, and increase our exhaustion.

In addition, the same applies to phone glances at bedtime. They open files and stop you sleeping; and you might also see some horrible covid updates and trigger a sleep-preventing churn.

Peas and Pythagoras don't mix

With all the demands you face at present, it is natural to try to maximize efficiency by doing different things at once. You think, I'll just put dinner on while I help with your schoolwork. In Pashler's research on dual-task interference, he showed that even when the tasks were quite different, doing two things at once makes you underperform in both. I've found, when I'm cooking and helping with homework, the peas get burnt and Pythagoras beats us. I am less present, the help I offer is less good and we both get frustrated. The same is true for your children and learning. When children study while media multitasking – WhatsApping friends, listening to music and watching TV – it reduces their learning recall and their academic performance[5] (even when they swear "that's how I learn best!").

2. Getting into flow

When we get really immersed in what we're doing, completely focused and absorbed, we get into a state of *flow*. This isn't easy to do in a noisy and distracting home. However, it really helps. A ten-year McKinsey study showed that executives were five times more productive when they were in flow; a flow state also increases creativity and learning,[6] and it's enjoyable.[7]

So how do we get immersed more frequently in the context of distractions? Daniel Gucciardi, an associate professor at the University of Western Australia, studied this in professional golfers. Those golfers who didn't just focus on what they were doing, but also thought about how they were swinging (e.g. 'smooth'), stayed immersed better in the face of distractions.[8]

We know that one of the predictors of a flow state is challenge. When we stretch ourselves we are more likely to immerse ourselves too. One of the things I find helpful, when working in noisy environments, is making my tasks harder. If I'm building a presentation, I'll challenge myself to make it surprising or beautiful. So, don't just do your work, challenge yourself. This extra challenge will help you immerse more fully, despite the noise.

Sudden outbreaks of silence

The World Health Organization estimated that, in Europe alone, one million years of life are lost due to noise pollution.[9] Excessive and persistent noise isn't just bad for performance and concentration, it's bad for everyone's stress and health. So, what can you do?

Professor of internal medicine at Italy's University of Pavia, Luciano Bernardi made an interesting finding. He was studying the effects of music on the cardiovascular system and relaxation. What he found surprised him. The greatest relaxation happened in the pauses between the 'relaxing' music. People relaxed most when silence broke out suddenly.

Noise is an essential ingredient of any family life. In fact, one of the things we loved most when we moved to Spain was the sheer volume of conversation in cafés. It spoke to us of joyful and exuberant togetherness. We all love that same exuberance in our family time together – just not all the time. Building on Bernardi's research, synchronise around noise levels. Take common breaks where volume of conversation and music erupts. Agree periods when calls can happen. However, agree on silent periods as well. In those moments collectively embrace sudden outbreaks of silence, where your home becomes a library. This will not just help you to concentrate, the contrast will help your stress levels as well.

3. Time and place

Time of the day matters when it comes to concentration. I already talked about parole judges, but the effects are seen in other walks of life too. For example, in hospitals we know that between 3 and 4 p.m., patients are three times more likely to be given a potentially fatal dose of anaesthesia[10] than between 9 and 10 a.m.!

We all have our best time of the day for concentration: some of us are morning types, others are night owls. However, the most common time for better concentration is the morning. That's why children who do tests in the afternoon have been shown to do 20 percent worse than those who do them in the morning.[11] Interestingly however, as our concentration dips, our creativity rises.[12] Concentration involves holding attention on a single thing for a long time. However, the very thing you need for creativity is connection-making. So, your tired, distracted brain might just be more imaginative.

So, when scheduling as a family, front-load your day with silence and focused activities. That's when to do your deep concentration, and to teach maths and the sciences. Then, as the day wears on, allow more noise, do more conference calls and get more creative and artistic.

Change places

One of the things that always surprises me is how often, even in flexible, open-plan offices, people gravitate to exactly the same place to work. For me, it's self-evident that different types of activity benefit from different surroundings. There are times I want to work in a library (for deep thinking), a coffee shop (for low-level productivity), at my white-board (for creativity and sense-making) and standing up (for blasting emails and conference calls). Each of these environments helps me in different ways. Even though we are confined, if you work via a laptop, you probably still have a number of choices about where you can work. In particular, look for options that offer one of the following: silence (bedroom), background buzz (living room), creative zone (near the toys), an urgent posture (kitchen stool). Then move through your day, depending on the task and your mood.

DURATION

Distractions are a big performance killer. While studies have shown that working from home can improve performance by 13–22 percent by reducing the noise,[13] I suspect those houses were pretty quiet. Today, as we sit in our confinement, we are trying to work in an environment that has become an office for multiple companies, a school classroom and a playground, all at the same time. A steady flow of digital distractions encourage us to touch our phones 2,500 a day; and our anxiety levels bubble with the news of the escalating pandemic. It's a more perfect storm for distraction than any time in history. So how might we respond; how might we surf this tsunami of noise?

1. Switch Less

The average office worker shifts attention every three minutes.[14] At present, in households with children, I suspect that time period might be even shorter. Each time we move between tasks, the brain takes a little time and energy to reorientate itself to the new task. This is called the *switch cost*. University of Michigan professor David Meyer has found the impact of this is a 40 percent reduction in our productivity,[15] it is also exhausting. You might feel effective as you switch backwards and forwards between activities. You will even be 'rewarded' by small squirts of dopamine. Despite this, you are getting less done, thinking less well, and exhausting yourself.

Big-chunking
Your work will be better, your conversations richer and your days less stressful if you *big-chunk* your day. Trying to simultaneously perform our job, teach our children and run the home at the same

time means intense levels of task switching. The basic principle
of big-chunking is clustering similar activities together. It's much
less demanding to switch within the same domain of tasks. It's
easier to switch back and forth between household chores than
it is to switch between chores and contract writing. It's easier to
switch back and forth between emails and voice messages; than
between knocking out emails and writing a strategic report.

Of course, perfect chunking is impossible. The point is that any
small increases in the way we cluster our activities, and decrease
our shifts between domains, will help.

How could you increase the chunking of your daily activity?

Blaster or grazer

Another way of thinking about structuring your day, especially
when it comes to digital communication, is asking whether you
are a grazer or a blaster. Grazers have their email, social media
and WhatsApp open by default. Through the day, while working on paid work or on family activities, they graze on digital
messages, operating in the zone of continuous partial attention.
Of course, the consequence of this is that they are only able to
graze on work projects and family conversations too. Blasters,
on the other hand, intentionally go into email or their to-do
list, at set times. In those moments they blast through email
and messages, killing off these distractions, before returning to
the people and problems that matter most for decent chunks of
time; their Big 3.

Personally, I have three rules for blasting the inbox and other
micro-tasks:

- Choose specific times for blasting. For the rest of the day,
  the email is off and the task list goes unaddressed. You don't
  need a to-do list to tell you what's most important: you know
  that already (or, if you don't, it's not important).

- Time-limit the blasts. Give yourself a deadline, or even better, put a clock in front of you. This not only protects your time for the important stuff, it also creates urgency to your blasting.
- Stand up. I have a desk that winds up and down. I find it really helps accelerate my blasting if I stand up.

2. Avoiding distractions (those you can!)

How often do you switch tasks? Whatever the frequency you just guessed, I would wager you are underestimating it. A study published in the journal *Cyberpsychology, Behaviour, and Social Networking,* found that people underestimated their frequency of distraction by a factor of ten.[16] Our rate of task switching is worrying since professor of informatics at University of California, Gloria Mark, found that workers took an average of twenty-three minutes to recover from interruptions and return to their original task.[17]

Some distractions are unavoidable, after all there is a certain urgency to superhero capes. However, Mark found that 44 percent of distractions in offices are self-induced.[18] This is because distractions are tempting, even if they involve dead mice. In fact, one study found that people were less good at resisting a ping, ring or a Google search, than they were at resisting sex and chocolate! Packing the dishwasher suddenly becomes alluring when the alternative is to start drafting that annual report! No matter how many distractions are unavoidable, a lot of the hopscotching isn't driven by necessity. It's because, in the present moment, the simple and immediate is more attractive than the complex and longer-term activity.

Strong willpower

In studies of self-control, researchers found something interesting. Those with strong willpower were no better at resisting temptation when it stared them in the face, they just had better habits.[19] Those with strong willpower prioritised building good habits; habits that helped them avoid temptation. Put another way, those with strong willpower didn't eat more healthily by resisting plates of chocolate cake; they just made sure they didn't go to the supermarket hungry, and that their fridge was full of healthy food.

In another study by Gloria Mark, an organisation agreed to switch its email off for a week. That one change meant that at the end of the week, the workers were less stressed, switched tasks less, and they stayed focused on the big stuff for longer. If you want to be more focused, switch off your notifications on your computer and phone; and set up your working space so you are not distracted by how messy your house is, or able to see the children's TV show.

Even as you read this you are thinking two things:

- I know this already Tony, get onto some fresh ideas.
- I accept it's true but it doesn't apply to me.

It drives me crazy how many people know about turning off notifications or avoiding distractions, yet don't. If you haven't switched off your notifications, either you think your willpower is strong enough (in which case you're wrong) or you are accepting the distraction.

3. Embrace distraction!

I have been fortunate to work with Berthold Gunster, the hilariously innovative Dutch creativity guru. He developed the idea of *Omdenken* – flip-thinking. The central premise is simple but brilliant. Turn your thinking about issues upside down. Instead of seeing problems, see them as opportunities for creativity. In his words, "When you let go of what should be, you open the door to what could be." Instead of focusing on your wish that the children could be less distracting, how about embracing it! That your corona confinement will be distracting is inevitable but you do not have to see it as a problem. How about seeing this as an opportunity for some fun, for some creativity and for some special moments with your children?

To make my point, I've flipped my own thinking on distractions. As I have said above, the research tells us the best way to deal with distractions is to avoid them. What would it mean, instead, to embrace distractions. How about we turn our distractions into opportunities for rich attention. How might that work? Here's a couple of ideas I've just come up with but I'm sure you could do better (and BTW I'd love to hear your distraction-embracing, attention-enhancing ideas on Twitter @ tonycrabbe, #flippingdistraction).

The Attention Alligator

Your children will need your help and attention through the day, and this will not always be at convenient times. That's just life. However, you can reduce the disruption of these distractions, and make the subsequent conversations better, by delaying them. You can do this by choosing a children's toy. Let's say an old cuddly alligator. You explain to the children that this is the Attention Alligator. If anyone wants attention from anyone else while they are working – on schoolwork or paid work – they place the Attention Alligator on that person's table, without saying a word, and walk away. The receiver of the alligator then has a few minutes to finish what they were doing and switch their attention more gracefully. In return, they take the Attention

Alligator back to the giver and give them joyful and undivided attention.

'Attention Time'

Or here's an idea inspired by Kerkhof's 'worry time'. How about finding an old box and asking the children to decorate it. This will be the family's Attention Box. Next to the box, leave some slips of paper and coloured pens. Whenever children have a question, they write it on a slip of paper, or draw a picture. In doing so, they don't distract you and allow you to focus. Every hour (or thirty minutes) you take a break from work, and make a big show of opening the box, answering the questions and showering the children with the attention they want. This shouldn't be one-way either. You should also write your own requests or questions and post them in the box, and revel in the attention of your children too.

These exact ideas may not work for you but with a little imagination, there are things we can do to transform distractions into opportunities for quality attention, and maybe have some fun at the same time. Thanks Berthold!

SUMMARY FOR THINK@HOME

Direction

1. *Pre-commit*

   Do you make good decisions when you go to the supermarket hungry? In the *hot* state we choose the more tempting, easy tasks over hard ones. Pre-commit to what you will do tomorrow in a *cold* state. Eat that frog: focus for the first hour of your day on your biggest, scariest job.

2.   *What will I do next?*

Many times each day we encounter choice moments. We've just finished something else and we ask "What will I do next?" (WWIDN). Your answer in these moments will determine your impact. In your WWIDN moments, look first at your Big 3 (before checking your inbox or to-do list).

3.   *Review your progress*

Jerry Seinfeld is funny because he has a big calendar and every day he writes jokes, he crosses off a day. He reviews progress against the activities that matter. Review your progress on your Big 3 at the end of each day. A sense of making progress on the big stuff is an important motivator.

Depth

1.   *One thing at a time*

The brain can only do one thing at a time, but multitasking is more subtle than we think. The brain operates with open and closed files. Close your files at the end of meetings by identifying next steps. Don't pollute your brain by glancing at your phone when you know you can't answer it.

2.   *Getting into flow*

In distracting environments we increase our ability to immerse ourselves – getting into *flow* – through making our tasks more challenging. For example, aim to make this report surprising or encourage sudden outbreaks of silence: when peace reigns, we think better.

3. *Time and place*
    On the whole, most people do deep concentration better
    in the morning, and their brains are more scattered (and
    so more creative) in the afternoon. Front-load your heavy
    thinking. Also, deliberately change your working location
    to stimulate different types of thinking.

Duration

1. *Switch less*
    The average worker shifts attention every three minutes,
    which means they get less done and become more tired!
    Big-chunk your paid and family work into clusters of similar
    tasks. Be a blaster rather than a grazer: go into email for brief
    spurts, then close down notifications and focus!

2. *Avoiding distractions*
    People with strong willpower are no better at resisting
    temptation, they are just better at avoiding it! They have
    better habits to avoid the temptation of busyness! Turn off
    notifications, and don't put your laptop in a place where you
    are forced to look at the messy kitchen!

3. *Embrace distraction!*
    Instead of seeing distraction as a problem, use *Omdenken*
    or 'flip thinking' to turn the problem into an opportunity.
    How could you turn the distractions from your children
    into great opportunities for joint attention? Remember the
    Attention Box and the Attention Alligator?

Chapter 7

Succeed@Home

Lin Qingxuan is a cosmetics company from Shanghai that draws on traditional Chinese medicine. It has more than 300 retail stores and over 2,000 employees. As the coronavirus outbreak hit, half of Lin Qingxuan's retail stores had to be closed indefinitely. Sales plummeted by 90 percent.

So, they reimagined their business. Using the collaboration and retailing tools of DingTalk and Taobao, they focused on their digital business. The beauty advisors who had been displaced by the shop closures retrained as online influencers. It worked fantastically well, and sales started to climb.[1] In one live streaming event, for example, a single beauty advisor sold more in two hours than four retail stores in a week. Their influencers worked so well that Lin Qingxuan went from struggling to survive, to thriving: it achieved a 200 percent growth in year on year sales.[2]

The current crisis is creating huge challenges for businesses, employees and the self-employed around the world. It is also creating opportunities. This chapter is designed to help you think through your strategy for success through corona, so you don't just survive this chaos, but thrive.

LEVERAGING DISTANCE

How do you think you would be affected if they raised the ceiling of your office? You might think in terms of mood or light. What if I told you that one of the biggest effects would be on your creativity and big picture thinking?[3] What if I told you that just leaning back in your chair would make a difficult task or decision seem easier?[4]

These are two simple examples of the effect of *psychological distance*. In essence, when psychological distance increases, our thinking tends to become broader, more strategic and creative. We are less socially influenced.[5] As I mentioned in chapter 3, when we elevate our thinking to higher levels of construal, we are more able to see what matters, with clarity.

One of the gifts we are all receiving from our confinement is a period of enforced psychological distance from work. We are physically distant from our workplaces, and we are socially distanced from the norms of office life. This provides us with a unique chance to sit back and reflect strategically on our work and career.

This is also true if you are not working at present, for example if you are self-employed. While you face the terrible financial challenges of no work, you also face the need to ready yourself and your strategy for our emergence from this crisis – to a world, and customer expectations, that may have changed. This section will help you to leverage this distance.

1. What do you want?

The first place to start is to reflect on what you want. Too often, our priorities are driven by the adrenaline-fuelled urgency of daily demands. We get stuck in the problems and dramas of immediate pressures. Psychological distance can help us to clarify what matters to us, and what we really want.

Temporal distance

Psychological distance is also created by time. Temporal distance means looking at a situation from a distant time, in the past or the future. Like spatial distance, seeing things from another time often helps us see things more clearly. Here are three simple exercises to help you leverage the power of time.

Your commencement speech

If you've never watched Steve Jobs's commencement speech at Stanford, you should. It's had eleven million views for a good reason. In it, he tells three stories about his life and career, sharing examples of what he had achieved and the lessons he has learnt.

Imagine it's ten years in the future. You've been asked to give a commencement speech. What would you want to be able to say?

Reverse mentor yourself

Reverse mentoring has become increasingly popular. Seasoned and senior executives get mentored by graduates, fresh out of college. They help them to see things from a fresh and more digital perspective.

Think back to when you were beginning in your career or in your current organisation. You were a rookie, ignorant of many things but also with fresh dreams and perspectives. If your rookie self was mentoring you now, what advice would they give you?

Memento mori

Throughout history, artists would place a skull in their studio, a memento mori. It was designed to remind them that they would die, and so spur them to create, so they didn't reach the end of their life in regret. I wasn't sure if I should include this example, given how painfully present death is at the moment. However, it can be a powerful way to refocus on what really matters to you.

When I was twenty-nine, I had a shock. I was told I was going to die within a few months. For forty-eight hours Dulcie and I lived with that diagnosis, until tests proved the diagnosis incorrect. It was a terrible time; and it was 48 hours I have always been grateful for. Many of the good decisions that have steered our life since then came from that time.

If you had a shock that reminded you how finite life is, what would you do first? What would it clarify?

What do you love?

Gallup's research has consistently shown low levels of employee engagement across the world. Too many of us are going through the motions at work, albeit at 100mph. It is natural to think we have to change our jobs in order to find work more compelling but research by Amy Wrzesniewski, professor at Yale's School of Business, challenges this. She has developed a concept called *job crafting*, which involves employees deliberately shaping their work to make it more compelling. Most importantly, it works. When employees craft their jobs, their performance improves, their enjoyment improves and their resilience increases.[6]

There are three big focus areas in job crafting, which are the tasks that you do, the interactions you have and the meaning you experience at work.

So, what about your work?

Tasks: How could you align your work activities to spend a greater percentage of your time on the tasks you love?

Interactions: How could you build more meaningful, helpful or energising relationships with your colleagues or customers?

Meaning: How could you build a greater sense of meaning and social purpose into your work?

Now is a great time to reflect on what we love about our role.

When employees, from hospital cleaners to Google engineers, did this they found that small shifts in their roles could make a big impact on performance and satisfaction.

What do you want to contribute?

The Nobel Prize–winning economist Amartya Sen suggested that we should think of wealth not in terms of what we have but in terms of what we can do. I would argue a similar shift is possible for success. We should not think of our success as the rewards we get but in terms of what we can contribute. Or indeed, success is the degree to which your life and career is lived in line with your values. As we progress further through this crisis, we see more and more people contributing to their communities, living in line with their values.

Reflecting on your values, what do you want to contribute? What difference do you aspire to make in the world and in the lives of others? How will the world be a better place as a direct result of your work?

2. Strategic focus

Having spent some time reflecting on what you want, the next place to explore is your strategic focus. Where do you need to focus in order to achieve what you want?

A starting SWOT

SWOT is possibly the most used strategic tool. It stands for Strengths, Weaknesses, Opportunities and Threats. When you go through each of the categories, you're not just creating a big list, but asking which are the two or three most important factors.

When you think about your strengths and weaknesses, you do this *relative* to your competition. You might have a strength but if it's not better than your colleagues, it doesn't count strategically! When you think about your opportunities and threats, these are about the employment market that is relevant to you (your company, the job market or, if you're an entrepreneur, the marketplace for your product or service).

Since this can be challenging, you could use distance again. This time, interpersonal distance: put yourself in the shoes of others. Thinking about something from the perspective of another person can help us see things more clearly. So, choose someone whose opinion in business you respect, and who knows you and your context well. It may be a wise mentor or brilliant colleague. As you work through the SWOT, think about what they would say about you, your competition and the market in each case.

Strengths: Gallup found that only one in three people use their core strengths every day;[7] that's a ridiculous waste of our abilities. So, what are the strengths you have that are most valuable, relative to your competition?

Weaknesses: Where are you less strong than your competitive set? Honestly.

Opportunities: What opportunities do you see in your organisation or the wider market, as a direct result of this crisis but also in the longer term?

Threats: What threats do you see in your organisation or the wider market, as a direct result of this crisis but also in the longer term?

From your SWOT, what are the implications for your strategic focus:

- During your confinement?
- Over the coming year?

Clarify your strategic position

Strategic focus starts with clarifying your strategic position. This describes the kind of 'business you are in'. It applies for those working in multinationals to help you think about where you should focus most in your role as well as for entrepreneurs. Identifying your strategic position will help you clarify the activities to focus on, and work out the problems to solve in order to have most impact. Getting this kind of clarity is particularly important at present, since your time for work may be more squeezed than usual.

To simplify this, there are two main types of strategic position: audience-based and product-based. Of course, we all have audiences and products. However, strategic positioning helps you identify your *primary* focus; which helps us strategically focus.

Audience-based positioning

This strategic position involves offering a wide range of products or services to a very specific group of customers, like a private bank that targets a small selection of wealthy individuals. They focus first on the audience: gaining a deep understanding of their customers' needs, building strong relationships with them and offering a one-stop shop for what they need.

If you think this is the strategic position for you:

Clarify: Who is your core audience?

Focus: Understand your audience needs and build relationships.

Problems: Identify audience problems to solve for them.

Product-based positioning

This strategy is all about focusing first on your products or expertise in a specific area. It's about differentiating yourself through what you do. What capabilities or areas of expertise could you develop that would truly set you apart? What service could you develop or offer that uniquely fits a specific need in your organisation or market, or that's just downright cool?

If you think this is the strategic position for you:

Clarify: What is your core 'product'? (Your capability or expertise that is most valuable)

Focus: Develop your expertise and build a reputation around it.

Problems: Identify problems to solve based on your capabilities

What does this mean for me?

Clarifying your strategic position can help most people. For example, a sales person may choose to take an audience-based position by focusing on their most important customers and catering to their needs. Or they might take a product-based position, if they focus on a specific area or specialism, to develop deep expertise. Their sales approach would then be based heavily on product or market expertise.

My business has historically been an audience-based business: providing psychological consulting to very specific folk in multinationals. When my book *Busy* came out, it created another business stream: keynotes, workshops and consulting specifically around busyness. This is a product-based business. For a little while I straddled both businesses, and I struggled. In the end, Dulcie took over the *Busy* business; she has a stronger background in running product-based businesses. She now hires me to the *Busy* business, as a consultant! This leaves me free to focus on my audience-base, and my psychology.

Getting clarity of the type of business you are in is super-valuable in helping you identify where to primarily focus and the problems to solve.

3. From the abstract to the concrete

Being intentional about construal thinking isn't just about getting abstract. Higher levels of abstract thinking can help us see things clearly but if we want to translate that clarity into action, we also have to get more concrete. Here's how.

Goal setting

Years of research shows goal setting works.[8] So far you've reflected on what you want, and where you should place a strategic focus. To bring focus to your reflections, now clarify your goals. Make sure each goal is specific, rather than general; and that you are clear how you will know that it has been achieved or not. In other words, how you will measure it. Set goals like this for each of the following:

- What is your five-year goal?
- What is your goal for the next twelve months?
- What is your goal for your corona confinement?

Distant trade-off advice

As we discussed earlier, trade-offs are essential, but can also be difficult. To help you to focus your work and career, here's another popular strategic exercise. It will help you to make choices. In the context of your goals, to bring real strategic focus into your activity, what do you need to:

- Stop doing?
- Start doing?
- Do more of, or do better?
- Do less of, or do imperfectly?

As you think through these questions, be specific and concrete.

NEVER LET A GOOD CRISIS GO TO WASTE

Alibaba, the multinational e-commerce giant, ranked as the ninth most valuable company in the world in 2018, was a tiny outfit in 2002. Following the SARS pandemic in Asia between 2002 and 2004, people became more conscious of travel and human contact. Alibaba grew exponentially. More recently, the financial crisis of 2008 lead to the growth of the sharing economy, and companies such as Uber and Airbnb.[9]

Winston Churchill is reported to have said "Never let a good crisis go to waste." This section will help you think through how you can use this current crisis to drive innovation not only in your business, but also in how you work. .

1. What problem are you trying to solve?

Between 1990 and 1995, Mihaly Csikszentmihalyi, professor of psychology and author of *Flow*, led a team to study ninety-one exceptional individuals, including fourteen Nobel Prize winners. All ninety-one were chosen because they had made major contributions in their field. In particular, he wanted to understand how they achieved their great breakthroughs. What he found was counter-intuitive: finding the solution was easy, the hard part was finding the right problem to address. Once the problem had been discovered, the breakthrough happened quite rapidly.[10] Creativity starts with identifying great problems.

So, *what problems are you trying to solve?*

- In the current corona crisis?
- To meet your career and strategic goals?

Ask great questions

An important habit that creative people have is the practice of asking great questions. Here's some questions proposed in a brilliant Harvard Business Review article 'Breakthrough Thinking Inside the Box'.[11] I've adapted them for the coronavirus.

- How are our customers using our service differently during the crisis? (How is your company using you differently during the crisis?)
- What's the biggest hassle faced by customers in working with us through this crisis?
- Who else has addressed similar issues to those we're facing in the crisis?
- What customer needs have shifted most significantly as a result of the crisis?
- What crisis-related customer needs are we not meeting?

The questions above are business focused, but they can also be reframed to become more personal or career-related. For example: What's the biggest hassle about working with *you* at present?

2. Cultivating creativity

Creativity is a choice. We either decide to approach situations creatively, or we just try and get through them. This view is supported by neuroscience. Researchers scanned peoples' brain activation before a problem-solving test. They found that creativity started before the test. Those who ultimately came up with the most creative solutions entered the problem with their anterior cingulate cortex activated. Their brains were primed to play with options and switch approaches. In other words, they were primed for creativity. Those that came up with more mundane approaches, had not primed their brains.

Creativity starts with the decision to try to create. My advice is that we all choose to approach the corona crisis (and your ongoing careers) with all the creativity we can muster. It costs nothing and can be transformational.

Beyond the first idea

The simplest creative strategy is nothing more complex than the habit of coming up with more than one idea. So often in life, when faced with a problem, we think of what we should do. We come up with an idea that sounds sensible; and we do it. Creative people, on the other hand, don't stop at the first idea. When a first idea is identified, they put it to one side and ask themselves, "What other ideas can I come up with?" or even, "What would a completely different approach be?" This is the essence of the creative choice. In the coming months, we can't predict what will happen. We will need every ounce of our creativity to innovate our way through the unknown. So, at the very least, aim to generate three different ideas before choosing the best.

Omdenken again

Building on the philosophy of flip-thinking, once you are clear on what your problem is, you could start by asking "How could we turn it into an opportunity?" This is exactly what Lin Quinxuan did, as I mentioned at the start of the chapter.

Take one of the problems you have identified as a result of the coronavirus? How could you flip it? How might you reimagine it as an opportunity?

3. Try different things

The travel site Booking.com doesn't know what their customers want, and that is why they have been so successful. More accurately, they don't make the assumption that they know what will work best for their customers. They don't rely on their expertise, because they recognise that consumer preferences are changing so quickly. Instead, the company is based on what they call A/B testing. They run two simultaneous versions of almost everything and then see which works best. At any one time they have 1,000 different experiments running. As Stuart Frisby, former director of design, explained: "If it can be a test, test it. If we can't test it, we probably don't do it." Research by Evercore Group shows that Booking.com's testing "drives conversions across the whole platform at 2–3 times the industry average."[12] Which means a lot of revenue.

In an odd way, the covid crisis is like an A/B test for your work and your life. It is a forced test of an alternative. All we have to do is capture and learn from the results.

For example, what are you doing differently in:

- Your daily working habits?
- The way you collaborate?
- The way you work with customers?

In each case, reflect on what you normally do (condition A) and what you are currently doing because of the crisis (condition B). Then ask yourself "What is working better that could be applied after the crisis?"

You might go a step further and ask "What problems in your business are you in the dark about at present?" Rather than trying to identify the right solution, do a test. Try a few things and see what works best; then try some more things. When you can't rely on your expertise, test!

"Dad, I don't get it!"

I remember hearing about a business strategy session where senior executives worked through the complexity of their business data and developed a plan. They were tasked with creating a way of communicating that message that was simple and compelling. Then, what they had produced was tested. Unexpectedly (for the execs at least) a group of school children were brought into the conference. The execs had to pitch their strategy to the children. The feedback, I imagine, was forthright and valuable.

How about using this strategy at home, since that's our context these days. If you have children, you have an amazing, on-tap panel to test any of your ideas. Children are often much better than adult panels for the following reasons:

- Simplicity: you'll soon hear "I don't get it!' if you aren't brutally simple and clear.
- Engaging: their tolerance for the dull is zero.
- Building: children are amazing at the 'and' game, building on top of your idea.

BUILD YOUR BRAND

Working from home has historically been linked to lower rates of promotion.[13] Even though everyone is working from home, our confinement is a great time to reflect on what we're known for in our businesses. Our usual displays of busyness and presenteeism around the office will not be seen. Busyness, always a dumb brand, is an even less effective thing to be known for at the moment.

So how can you build your brand when you are less visible to everyone? I suggest we all use this chance to clarify what we stand for. It will help us cut through the noise of this crisis but it will serve us well, long after the virus has passed from the news into the archives.

1. Authenticity is key

An effective brand is authentic. When clarifying your brand, do not start by thinking about what your employer wants or values. Think about yourself. It starts by getting super-clear on two things: your values and your core strengths. Your values determine the person you strive to be. They are your core beliefs: what's important to you, and what is and isn't acceptable. They should form the foundation of your brand because they are what you really care about, and therefore what you want to stand for.

Core strengths

Your brand isn't just a summary of your skills, it's you at your absolute best. It should be true and authentically you but on a really good day.

To clarify your core strengths, identify three times over the last year or so, when you were at your absolute best. Where you made a real impact. Don't simply jump to your biggest successes; we have probably all had experience of pulling off a massive deal, even though we definitely were not at our best. Identify times when what you did was you at your best: your approach, your handling of a situation, your intervention or ideation. This is about surfacing your core strengths, so identify times when you were awesome!

To clarify the occasions to focus on, you could choose a six-month project, that really brought out the very best of your skills. Or it might have been a short corridor conversation, where you said something that made a huge impact on the other person. Reflect on these times and ask yourself the following questions:

- What specifically did you do?
- What did you do that made the most impact?
- What are the themes across your three examples?

The idea of this exercise is to help you clarify when you are at your absolute best; your core strengths. This will help you build a brand that focuses on your most powerful contribution to your business or the world.

2. Clarify your brand

Who would you invest in? A company listed on the New York Stock Exchange with the three-letter ticker symbol of 'KAR' or one listed as 'RDO'? It turns out, if you had invested in KAR you would have made 9 percent more money than if you had chosen RDO.[2] This is an example of *cognitive fluency*. Cognitive fluency is the degree to which a mental task is easy or hard work. When things are easy for the brain to process, we like them more, trust them more and choose for them more.[3] Which is why we don't like people who use big words; we trust rhyming statements; and when Procter and Gamble gave people fewer versions of Head & Shoulders to choose from, its overall sales for the shampoo went up.[4]

A good personal brand should be brutally clear and simple. Think of Volvo. There is a huge amount of technology in those cars, and a big range. Yet Volvo have reduced their brand down to a single word: 'safe'. You are a complex person, with lots of skills and experiences. However, everyone making decisions about you is furiously busy. The simpler you can make it for people to understand your core contribution to the business the better. If you make it easy for people to 'get' you, with a clear and simple brand, they will like you more, trust you more and decide for you more.

So, what is your brand?
There are three steps to establishing your brand:

- Identify your core values and strengths (we covered these earlier in the chapter as well as in chapter 3). Any brand should be based on these.
- Reflect on your values and strengths, asking yourself this question: "What is my most powerful contribution?" Identify one or two core elements of your brand. These may come from your core values or core strengths (or both).
- Decide how you will express the core elements of your brand. What is your brand statement? The most important thing is that your brand statement should feel authentic to you; something you'd be comfortable telling people.

Salesforce is an amazing company, and a fast one. The speed of their growth over the last decade has meant that people have to work at pace. I have done a lot of work over the years with high potential leaders there. They recognize the importance of brand when everyone around them is busy, and when a lot of work is done virtually. Here are some examples of what they came up with to give you an idea of what a brand statement looks like: "I ...

- make the complex, simple."
- join the dots." (you're great at connecting people and ideas)
- am all about people."

- am a marathon runner." (you pride yourself on ridiculous levels of resilience)
- am Nike with soul." (you have a 'Just Do It' focus combined with strong values)

3. Construct your brand

When it comes to building your brand, here are five focus areas for when you're working from home. Don't do all of them but use these strategies to identify what will work best for you and your brand.

The drop
A drop is nothing more than inserting your brand into a conversation or presentation, in a way that feels natural and informal.

- In a presentation if you have made a point about connecting people and ideas, you might say, "You see, I'm all about *joining the dots.*"
- Or comment on why something matters to you, "As you know, I'm *all about energy.* We have to figure out how to bring more energy into this."

Living up to your brand
If your brand is you at your best, intentionally doing it more should be a good thing. For example, if your brand is 'clarity', constantly challenge yourself to live up to it.

- Look for chances to innovate by making business processes more clear (you could even call it 'Project Clarity').

- In meetings, be the person who summarises the chaos, saying, "So, for clarity, the three key points so far are ..."

Digital
What is your digital presence through your confinement?

If your brand is expertise-based, how about starting a blog or actively sharing articles via the company's social media. Just make sure of two things: the articles are relevant to your brand and they are useful to the audience.

If your brand is relationship-based, you could arrange some virtual coffee catch-ups to maintain and build connections.

As I mentioned before, do not try to do all of these strategies. Just choose one or two ways to build your brand during your confinement in a way that is effective but also feels authentic. Remember, you have a reputation whether you like it or not; your choice through this confinement, is whether you want to turn those views into a powerful brand.

SUMMARY FOR SUCCEED@HOME

Leveraging distance

1. *What do you want?*
   Use temporal distance to give perspective about what you want: what would your old self, and future self, advise? How might you *job craft* your way to more motivation by shifting the tasks, the interactions and the meaning in your work. Also, what do you want to contribute?

2.   *Strategic focus*
      Carry out a SWOT analysis on your career. What are your
      strengths, weaknesses, opportunities and threats? What
      is your strategic position: is it audience or product-based?
      Then determine where you should focus, and what prob-
      lems you should solve.

3.   *From abstract to concrete*
      High level construal thinking is good for clarity, but to get
      into action, it helps to get more concrete. Set specific goals
      for what you want to achieve. How do you need to focus to
      deliver these: what do you need to start or stop; what should
      you do better, and more imperfectly.

Never let a good crisis go to waste

1.   *What problem are you trying to solve?*
      Nobel Prize-winners found their breakthrough came easily
      once they had identified the right problem to solve. So, what
      problem do you want to solve? Ask great questions to frame
      your thinking, for example,"What's the biggest hassle about
      working with you at the moment?"

2.   *Cultivating creativity*
      Creativity starts with the decision to be creative. When
      people have the intent to be creative, different parts of
      their brain is activated. Get into the habit of going beyond
      the first idea, generate at least three! And flip problems into
      opportunities – Omdenken them!

3. *Try different things*

    When we don't know the right answer, do what Booking.
    com does: try different things! Experiment with different
    options and keep what works best. See this whole period
    as an A/B test. Compare your covid habits with your usual
    practices: what works best, and how can you learn from this
    after the crisis?

Build your brand

1. *Authenticity is key*

    Busy is a rubbish brand, because it's boring and doesn't
    differentiate you. Build your brand on your values (what
    you care about) and your core strengths. Remember, your
    brand isn't just a summary of you; it's you at your best, on a
    really good day.

2. *Clarify your brand*

    The brain likes things super-simple. It mixes up *cognitive
    fluency* (how easy something is to process) with other
    judgements. When something is clear and simple, the brain
    likes it, trusts it and chooses it more. That's why Volvo has
    build their brand on a single word: 'safe'. So even though
    you are a complex person with a rich history; make your
    brand brutally simple.

3. *Construct your brand*

    There are three simple ways to build your brand from a
    distance. The drop: mention your brand in a natural way
    in conversation. Live up to your brand: intentionally act
    consistently with your brand (you at your best). Develop a
    digital strategy: start a blog or go for a virtual coffee.

Chapter 8

Evolve@Home

Between 1347 and 1351 the Black Death ravaged Europe, killing millions. Ralph Higden, a chronicler of the middle ages, wrote that "scarcely a tenth of mankind was left alive ... There were hardly enough living to care for the sick and bury the dead".[1] In the middle of the crisis, it was almost inconceivable that it would ever pass; but it did.

Terrible though those four years were, great things happened as a result of the Black Death. Repressive social structures that had existed for centuries were washed away. History professor Tom James, from the University of Winchester, explains that one of the biggest outcomes of the Black Death was the dismantling of the feudal system that had been in place for 600 years. In this system of rank and privilege, only those at the top had a good deal. At the bottom of the social ladder, peasants had to work their lord's land, and pay rent for the right to live on it too! They were subject to harsh taxes and capricious judgements from their master. Following the Black Death, the value of labour massively increased. It gave power back to the peasants and dislodged the unquestionable authority of the ruling classes. The land owners had to start attracting workers.

Much better employment terms were needed, improving conditions and overall freedom. Life, in short, became much better for the majority of people. As living conditions improved across the continent, so society progressed. For example, some scholars suggest that the Black Death – particularly devastating in Italy – contributed to the flourishing of the Renaissance[2] the following century.

We can be confident of three things about the coronavirus: it is terrible, it will pass, and it will lead to great things. This chapter is designed to be read as you prepare to leave confinement, and transition back into 'normal' or at least, post-corona life. It's a chance to reflect on the challenges you have faced on your journey but also on the positive things that have come from this period. This is designed to help you look at your corona confinement as a unprecedented experiment in a different life, and extract learnings that could lead to great things.

WHAT DID YOU LEARN?

As Havard behavioural scientist, Francesca Gino, showed in her research, when we reflect, our learning and performance increases by 23 percent. So, it would seem crazy to exit our isolation without taking the time to reflect on the experiences that helped us thrive in confinement, to enable us to thrive through life for years to come.

This reflection is designed as a conversation to have with your family, your partner or even a friend. It is based on Martin Seligman's 'better-than-Prozac' three best things exercise. Doing this with at least one other person has three benefits:

- It makes it a richer reflection: we tend to reflect more deeply when we do it with someone else.

- Hearing what the other person says will also help you to reflect and learn; their memories will trigger you.
- These discussions build commitment and accountability for carrying these behaviours forward after the crisis.

1. Best things

Over your confinement you have done a lot of things. Sensible things, boring things and silly things. Some of those will have had an impact: helping you do great work, soothing your child's anxiety or supporting your mum. Some of those things will have kept you sane or healthy, and the family together. This is your chance to reflect on what worked best. Which activities and actions would be first on your list of advice to someone about to enter confinement?

The way this conversation works

- Each person shares their three best things for the first question.
- Everyone asks questions and makes listening noises! Curiosity is key.

The first questions:
Over the confinement, what were the best things you did . . .

1. with the family?
2. by yourself?
3. in your work/schoolwork?

Each time, ask the person to name their three and explain why they were the best.

Then, together discuss the following questions:

- What were your biggest learnings from the above?
- What do you want to continue after confinement?

2. Best moments

Happiness isn't just to be found in the things we do but in the moments we share, shafts of luminous togetherness and joy. These might include flow experiences, butterfly moments or great conversations.

Over the period of our confinement, what were your three best . . .

1. moments?
2. conversations?
3. days?

These can be work- or family-related. Each time, ask the person to explain why they were the best.

Again, together discuss the following:

- What did you learn from these?
- What do you want to continue after confinement?

3. Best habits

One of the big things you had to do was to put in place new habits, for work and within the family. Habits matter for our success and happiness. We might see this whole period as a great big experiment in new habits, as long as we take the time to reflect on the results.

What were the best three habits and routines . . .

1. we had as a family?
2. you had for your work or school?
3. for your health or happiness?

Then, together discuss the following questions:

- What were your biggest learnings from the above?
- What do you want to continue after confinement?

Finally discuss:

- What were the big insights from this conversation?
- What were the big surprises?
- What do we commit to do as a result?

WHAT DID YOU LEARN ABOUT YOU?

So far we've reflected on what you did. Now let's go a little deeper. What did you learn about yourself through this process?

1. Resilience

We'll start by reflecting on how well you coped with the challenges of the last few months. I'll focus on resilience because it really matters in a world that suddenly feels a little more uncertain.

The most common definition of resilience is positive adaptation in the face of adversity.[3] Since the experience of going through crises builds our resilience, you should reflect on the secret of your success over the corona crisis. What did you do that helped you to adapt and persist positively? What lessons can you learn from this that will be helpful as you face future challenges in your life?

The last weeks and months have been tough, but we have faced adversity, and we have prevailed.

Purpose
One of the most powerful ways people are able to persist in the face of adversity is when they have a sense of purpose. Our ability to find meaning in the midst of the challenge, using our values as guides through the crisis. Remember Alessia Bonari, the Italian nurse from chapter 5? When she put on her painful mask each day and faced the horrors and personal threat of the virus at the frontline, she wasn't motivated by her paycheck or the hope of a promotion. She continued to care in the face of discomfort, distress and danger, because her work had meaning to her. She had a purpose; she was making a contribution that mattered.

What about you?
Joseph Campbell, who was a professor of literature and mythology, explains that just about all literature represents a single story. He captured this idea best in his book *The Hero with a Thousand Faces*. Every story, from *Star Wars* to *Sleeping Beauty*, represents mankind's journey through adversity. As the hero accepts, faces and overcomes their challenges, they reach the treasure.

The treasure we gain from adversity is clarity. Adversity is an acid test. It helps us clarify what really matters to us. When everything else is stripped away, when tribulation tears at our resolve, those few things that shine through the gloom are our gold that lies at the end of our journey.

Reflect on your journey through the covid crisis. Answer the following questions:

- What motivated you through the period and kept you going when it was really tough?
- What gave your work, teaching and care meaning?
- What does this experience say about you? What does it tell you about what really matters to you? What is your treasure?

Positivity

Learned optimism is one of the central aspects of resilience. This optimism isn't blind positivity, denying any negative views or realities. In fact, such blind positivity has a negative effect. It is three things: the persistent focus on activities that are within our control; the acceptance of things that are not; and the ability to reframe situations in a positive manner.

We've discussed these ideas earlier in the book. What I want to focus on here is the *learned* part of learned optimism. In particular, what you can learn from your actions and explanations through this crisis that can help you to be optimistic again as you face future challenges.

Reflect on the following questions:

- What did you do that helped you to focus on what was within your control, despite your worries?
- What did you have to accept in your life and about yourself, through this crisis? How did you manage this?
- How did you reframe situations positively, when everything seemed bleak, to help yourself or others see the bright side?

People

The third 'p' of resilience is people. It is about reflecting on the people who supported you and were most central and essential to your journey. The strength of our support networks are possibly our greatest source of resilience. Friends are vital for our wellbeing and happiness, as well as our family relationships and work engagement.[4] They help us face, and even smile through, adversity. For example, we are thirty times more likely to laugh when talking to friends,[5] and we know laughter is a great stress reducer!

Over your confinement, you probably found that certain people rose to the surface. Among your family members and friends, there were a few who supported and energised you the most, who you learned to lean on more than the others.

Of all your friends and family:

- Whose support was most valuable for you? What needs did they help you to meet?
- Who did you help most? How? How did helping them help you?
- How will you acknowledge your most valuable supporters now the crisis is over?

2. Busyness

Busyness is a gentle poison that destroys our work, lives and relationships from the inside out. As we bounce and juggle our many demands with a constant stream of messages and micro-demands, our thinking dies along with our impact. As we race and cram our way through over-stuffed agendas, we burn through our energy and in our exhaustion our lives feel grey. As we perforate our relationships with email and WhatsApp, we skate over the surface of our conversations rather than dive into them, we press pause on our love in favour of 'likes'.

One of our opportunities through this crisis has been to experiment with a different way of working and living. To try new habits and choices, away from the social norms of our offices. To try a different way of working in an environment where we set the rules. In doing this, we will learn what works better, but we may also realise something else: our office and manager are not to totally to blame for our busyness; a lot of it comes from us.

To help you reflect on your busyness, think about what you have learned across five domains of busyness. I'll outline the domains first, and then ask the reflection questions.

Busy as a choice
Busyness is a choice, or more accurately a lack of choice. It is trying to do everything for everyone, and failing to make the tough trade-off choices. It is choosing the immediate and urgent over what really matters.

Busy as reactivity
A significant aspect of busyness is endless reactivity, a life driven by your inputs, rather than your desired outputs; where the inbox and micro-tasks are focused on more than your values and your Big 3.

Busy as a lack of depth
Busyness is shallow processing. It is a lack of full and deep attention. Where we struggle to concentrate, in the moment, on the people or the problems that matter.

Busy as distraction
Busyness is the rapid hopscotching between activities, distracted by our pings and rings.

Busy as always 'on'
Busy is the inability or unwillingness to switch off, where evenings, meals and family conversations are perforated with glances and grabs for your phone.

For each one of these five domains of busyness (choice, reactivity, depth, distraction and always on):

- What did you do well over this period?
- What did you not do well?
- What can you learn about yourself from this?

Overall, what are the biggest one or two lessons about your relationship with busyness that you should take back into your life beyond covid?

3. Learning from your failures

There will have been aspects of your life in confinement where, despite your best efforts, you failed. When you knew what you wanted to do, in your work or with your family, and yet couldn't make it happen. When day after day, you just could not seem to make your good intentions turn into action. Or if you did, once or twice, you soon fell back into old habits. You perhaps didn't live up to your aspirations in work, as a parent or in your health. For example, you might have persistently struggled to switch off, even though you knew you should. You might not have exercised, or your teaching efforts might have been limp at best.

If you recognise this situation, if your motivation, your techniques and reminders didn't help you to follow through on your intentions, there is something to learn from that. It might be an *adaptive problem*. Adaptive problems are not solved through tools and techniques. What stops us succeeding and following through on our intentions is not a lack of sticky-note reminders. It is our beliefs and emotions.

For example, a friend of mine wanted to start running again. He was turning sixty and wanted to feel young. Half a lifetime ago he had been a competitive runner. For years he had been frustrated by his inability to rebuild the habit of running. He'd tried all of the techniques he could to motivate himself to train. Finally, he came to a moment of realisation: when he ran, it made him feel old, and it disgusted him. In other words, he wanted to run to feel young but the act of running made him feel old! Not surprisingly he struggled to persist. However, once he had this insight he could experiment, and even be playful with it. Now, when he runs, he doesn't just record his pace on Strava, he records the age he felt!

When looking at yourself and your corona confinement:

- What was one behaviour or habit you were committed to, but persistently failed to do?
- What was the pattern of thoughts and feelings that occurred just before each failure, specifically?
- What need might your beliefs or feelings be serving?

Deep-seated beliefs or emotions don't change overnight. They are often a product of childhood. The starting point is self-awareness. Once we are clear of the pattern of thoughts and feelings we experience, our focus for change shifts from tactics and reminders. We recognise it is we, ourselves, who are the problem.

To make change in these areas, we don't solve, we move through. Those feelings and beliefs might always remain, but they don't have to hold us hostage. We can start intentionally experimenting with behaviours that run counter to our beliefs or emotions. You will still feel those emotions, but they no longer control you.

If, through your confinement, a few adaptive problems have surfaced in your life, you have made real progress. They have the power to teach you lessons about yourself that are deep and valuable.

LEARNING FORWARD

Of course, there will come a day (hopefully very soon) when our confinement stops. This section is about how we can take all this great learning and incorporate it into our post-covid life.

1. What are you going to change?

If you want to change something, or create a new habit, there is a crucial place to start. With crystal clarity. For example, we know that when people are specific on not just the behaviour they want to change, but also the location and time when they will perform this behaviour, they are much more likely to do it.[6]

For example, imagine you want to exercise every day through your confinement, instead of saying to yourself "I want to exercise more", say "Every morning I'll go straight into the living room to do a *PE with Joe* workout session."

On a more work-related example, instead of saying "I will be less distracted by emails", say "I will spend the first working hour each day focused on my Big 3. Email notifications will be switched off, and my phone will be out of sight."

If-then

Sometimes we can't predict the location or the time of a target behaviour. However, it still helps to get pretty specific. This is called the *If-then* technique. For example, instead of saying "I'll do less work in the evenings", we say "*If* I receive a meeting invite for a call after 6 p.m. then I will reply, asking if it can be rescheduled during office hours." Amazingly, of those who came up with If-then plans for exercise, 91 percent stuck to them. Of those who didn't, only 39 percent carried on exercising.[7]

2. Increasing your odds of success

Here are a few additional ideas to help you increase your odds of success.

Reverse-engineer your habits

In chapter 2, you reflected on your pre-covid rhythms and the needs they were serving. Now do the same with your confinement rhythms.

- Write out your typical, confinement workday routine.
- Now compare this with your pre-covid routines. Decide which elements work best from each list, and why.
- Craft your new and improved post-confinement routine.

It will be remarkably easy to slip into old routines and unhelpful habits. So be intentional from day one. Establish your revised routine immediately and craft your new habits onto the framework of your routine.

Creating the anchors

The most obvious anchors that you will need to focus on, as you recraft your routines, are those you have at the start and end of your work day: leaving home, starting work, finishing work and arriving home. I strongly suggest you over-focus on anchoring any new behaviours to these. For example, starting your day with your Big 3, or disconnecting in the evening.

Pre-commit

I gave an example of getting specific about the what, when and where of your desired behaviour. The example I gave was exercising. You'll increase the odds of this behaviour sticking even further if you pre-commit. Leave your exercise gear next to your bed and set up your iPad so the next *PE with Joe* is ready to play!

Use social influence

At Newcastle University, employees were expected to pay for their drinks, and so an honesty box was left. Above the prices, an image was placed, of either a set of eyes, or flowers. In the weeks when flowers were shown, the average contribution paid for a litre of milk was 15p. In the weeks that the eyes were displayed, that figure more than quadrupled to 70p.[8]

What set of eyes do you want to have pointed at you as you try to change your behaviour? Who will hold you accountable? Your co-confiners might be the perfect people. You might also ask a colleague at work to watch you and nudge you if you slip.

3. ... and "hello world!"

In our absence, the world has had a chance to breathe. Fish have returned to the canals of Venice, New York's pollution levels have dropped by 50 percent, dolphins have been seen swimming off the coast of Mumbai, and endangered olive ridley turtles are again day-nesting on the beaches of Odisha. In fact, on 8th March, Stanford environmental economist Marshall Burke estimated that the reduced air pollution in China would probably save 70,000 lives.[9] That figure, one assumes, will now be dramatically higher.

As we emerge back into the world, it's up to each of us to bring the lessons and the wisdoms of this period with us. Who hasn't watched travel shows during this confinement with a sense of awe at the size, diversity and wonder of our planet? Who hasn't felt humbled by the displays of warmth, generosity and humanity of our communities? I never thought I'd see the day when wild pigs would roam the streets of a deserted Paris. Or when the prime minister of New Zealand, Jacinda Ardern, would describe the Easter bunny and the tooth fairy as essential key workers, not subject to the lockdown. These are strange, terrifying but magical times. Every generation faces its challenges and its opportunities. Each generation has a moment that defines them. After we have survived our corona crisis, the question we have to ask ourselves is "What next?" Do we emerge unchanged by this period, or do we evolve? Do we allow our renewed awe and togetherness to guide us on a better path? I can't help wondering whether perhaps – just perhaps – this might be our moment.

SUMMARY FOR EVOLVE@HOME

What did you learn?

1. *Best things*

   Reflection improves learning and performance. So, take the time to reflect on the three best things you did as a family, in yourself and in your work or schoolwork. Then let everyone reflect together on the big learnings and what you want to continue doing after the crisis.

2. *Best moments*

   Happiness isn't just to be found in the things we do, but in the moments we share, shafts of luminous togetherness and joy. So, reflect on the best moments, the best conversations, and the best days of your confinement.

3. *Best habits*

   Habits matter for our success and happiness. If we see this whole period as a great big experiment in new habits, what were our best habits as a family, in our work or schoolwork, and for our health and happiness?

What did you learn about you?

1. *Resilience*

   One of the gifts of tribulation is clarity of purpose, that is your treasure. What did you learn about what really mattered to you? How did you stay positive and focused on what's within your control? Who were the people who supported you most; how did you support them?

2. *Busyness*
    This has been a unique chance to experiment with our busyness away from office social norms. Reflect on what you learned about your busyness across five domains: busy as a choice, busy as reactivity, busy as a lack of concentration, busy as distraction and busy as always 'on'.

3. *Learning from your failures*
    When we persistently try to do something, and keep failing to follow through, it might be an adaptive problem. If it is, we don't need techniques as such to address it. We need to change our beliefs and emotions. What adaptive problems surfaced for you in your confinement?

Learning forward

1. *What are you going to change?*
    Get clear on what you will change but also where and when you will do this. The more specific you are the better. For behaviours that are more reactive, try the If-then strategy: "If I get a meeting request for after 6 p.m., then . . ." It more than doubles your chances of success.

2. *Increasing your odds of success*
    Connecting new behaviours to established habits improves success rate, integrate what was good about your confinement routine with your pre-covid habits. Particularly focus on the anchors. Then pre-commit to key behaviours and use social influence to keep you on track.

3. *... and "hello world!"*

With wild pigs on the streets of Paris, and the Easter bunny listed as a key worker, who knows what will happen next! Do we emerge unchanged by this period, or do we evolve? Do we allow our renewed awe and togetherness to guide us on a better path? It's your choice.

Notes

Preface

1. K. Lanaj, C. H. Chang, and R. E. Johnson, "Regulatory Focus and Work-Related Outcomes: A Review and Meta-Analysis," *Psychological Bulletin* 138, no. 5 (September 2012): 998–1034.
2. Michelle F. Davis and Jeff Green, "Three Hours Longer, the Pandemic Workday Has Obliterated Work-Life Balance," Bloomberg, April 23 2020
3. Ibid.
4. J. Stoeber and D. P. Janssen, "Perfectionism and Coping with Daily Failures: Positive Reframing Helps Achieve Satisfaction at the End of the Day," *Anxiety, Stress, & Coping* 24, issue 5 (October 2011): 477–97.

Chapter 1: *Mindset@Home*

1. S. F. Maier and M.E.P. Seligman, "Learned Helplessness: Theory and evidence," *Journal of Experimental Psychology: General* 105, no. 1 (1976): 3–46.
2. Amy F. T. Arnsten, "The Biology of Being Frazzled," *Science* 280, no. 5370 (June 12, 1998): 1711–12.
3. Victor E. Frankl, *Man's Search for Meaning* (London: Rider Books for Ebury Publishing, 2004).
4. Anna Phelan (2020), ("Is your to-do list making you nuts? Start a to-don't list instead" — with inspiration from author Adam Grant), Ideas.TED.com, (March 7, 2020)
5. Ibid.
6. Erik Helzer and Eranda Jayawickreme 'Control and the "Good Life": Primary and Secondary Control as Distinct Indicators of Well-being'. Social Psychological and Personality Science DOI: 10.1177/1948550615576210 (2015).
7. Brené Brown, *Daring Greatly: How the Courage to Be Vulnerable Transforms the Way We Live, Love, Parent, and Lead* (New York: Gotham Books, 2012).
8. Professor Robert E Kelly BBC interview about South Korean politics is interrupted by his children https://www.youtube.com/watch?v=Mh4f9AYRCZY.
9. Aronson, E., Willerman, B., & Floyd, J., "The effect of a pratfall on increasing interpersonal appeal," *Psychonomic Science* (1966)

10. Deaux, K., "To err is humanizing: But sex makes a difference," Representative Research in Social Psychology, 3, (1972): 20–28.

11. Deborah Spar, *Wonder Women: Sex, Power, and the Quest for Perfection* (New York: Sarah Crichton Books, 2013).

12. Glassdoor Covid-19 Poll conducted by The Harris Poll https://www.glassdoor. com/employers/blog/new-survey-covid-19/.

13. "Multitasking: Switching costs," American Psychological Association, March 20, 2006, http://www.apa.org/research/action/multitask.aspx.

14. Barbara L. Fredrickson, "What Good Are Positive Emotions?" *Review of General Psychology* 2, no. 3 (1998): 300–19.

15. M. Losada and E. Heaphy, "The Role of Positivity and Connectivity in the

16. Performance of Business Teams: A Nonlinear Dynamics Model," *American Behavioural Scientist* 47 (2004): 740–65.

(*Note:* There has been some questioning of the accuracy of some of the complicated mathematics behind this ratio. It's not worth worrying about the specific number, but the principle of the ratio of positive to negative still holds.)

17. John Gottman, *What Predicts Divorce?* (Hillsdale, NJ; Lawrence Erlbaum Associates, Inc., 1994).

18. E. J. Masicampo and R. F. Baumeister, "Consider it Done!: Plan Making Can Eliminate the Cognitive Effects of Unfulfilled Goals," *Journal of Personality and Social Psychology* 101, no. 4 (2011): 667–83.

19. Ad Kerkhof, *Stop Worrying: Get Your Life Back with CBT* (Berkshire, England: Open University Press, 2010).

20. Joe Brownstein, "Planning 'Worry Time' May Help Ease Anxiety," *LiveScience*, July 26, 2011, http://www.livescience.com/15233-planning-worry-time-ease-anxiety.html.

21. Michael J. Apter, *Reversal Theory: Motivation, Emotion and Personality* (Florence, KY: Routledge, 1989).

Chapter 2: *Rhythms@Home*

1. https://www.youtube.com/watch?v=HezxInuN1YA

2. Salimpoor, VN; Benovoy, M; Larcher, K; Dagher, A; Zatorre, RJ (2011). "Anatomically distinct dopamine release during anticipation and experience of peak emotion to music". *Nature Neuroscience*. 14 (2): 257–62.

3. Laura M Lyall et al, "Association of disrupted circadian rhythmicity with mood disorders, subjective wellbeing, and cognitive function," *The Lancet*, Volume 5, Issue 6, (2018): 507–514.

4. H Isabella Lanza and Deborah Drabick, "Family Routine Moderates the Relation Between Child Impulsivity and Oppositional Defiant Disorder Symptoms." *Journal of Abnormal Child Psychology*, 39, (2011): 83–94.

5. David T. Neal, Wendy Wood, and Jeffrey M. Quinn "Habits – A Repeat

Performance," *Current Directions in Psychological Science*, vol 15: 4, (2006): 198–202.

6. Daniel Kahneman, *Thinking, Fast and Slow* (New York: Farrar, Straus and Giroux, 2012).

7. Michael Slepian et al, "The Cognitive Consequences of Formal Clothing," *Social Psychological and Personality Science* (2015).

8. Matthew Hutson, Tori Rodriguez (2016) "Dress for Success: How Clothes Influence Our Performance.' *Scientific American*, (January 1, 2020).

9. Linda Stone coined the term "Continuous Partial Attention" in 1998, http://lindastone.net/qa/continuous-partial-attention.

10. Juliett Jowitt (2016) "Work-life balance: flexible working can make you ill, experts say." The *Guardian*, (January 2, 2020).

11. Victoria Sayo Turner (2016) "The Strain of Always Being on Call," *Scientific American*, (January 5, 2020).

12. Brian Wansink, James E. Painter, and Jill North, "Bottomless Bowls: Why Visual Cues of Portion Size May Influence Intake," *Obesity Research* 13, no. 1 (January 2005): 93–100.

13. Leslie A. Perlow and Jessica L. Porter, "Making Time Off Predictable—and Required," *Harvard Business Review* 87, no. 10 (October 2009): 102–9, 142.

14. Brandon Smit "Successfully leaving work at work," *Journal of Occupational and Organisational Psychology*, 89, (2015): 493–514.

15. Marc G. Berman, Jon Jonides, and Stephen Kaplan, "The Cognitive Benefits of Interacting with Nature," *Psychological Science* 19, no. 12 (2008): 1207–12.

16. Linda Stone, "Diagnosis: Email Apnea," *Linda Stone* (blog), November 30, 2009, http://lindastone.net/2009/11/30/diagnosis-email-apnea.

17. B. C. Madrian and D. F. Shea, "The Power of Suggestion: Inertia in 401(k) Participation and Savings Behavior," *The Quarterly Journal of Economics* 116, issue 4 (2001): 1149–87.

18. Julie Olson-Buchanan and Wendy Boswell, "Blurring boundaries," *Journal of vocational behaviour.* 68, (2005): 432–445.

19. Daniel Kennedy et al, "Personal space regulation by the human amygdala," *Nature.* 12: (2009): 1226–1227.

20. Daniel Wegner, *White bears and other unwanted thoughts: Suppression, obsession and the psychology of mental control* (Guilford Press, 1994).

21. Brigit Katz. "How to Avoid Passing Anxiety on to Your Kids," Child Mind Institute (Mar 2020).

22. Rae Jacobson. "Supporting Kids During the Coronavirus Crisis" Child Mind Institute (Mar 2020).

23. Wei-chinHwang "Practicing Mental Strengthening: Learning Effective Thinking Strategies" in *Culturally Adapting Psychotherapy for Asian Heritage Populations* (2016).

Chapter 3: *Choose@Home*

1. John M Grohol (2020), "Panic buying" *Psych Central*, (March 19, 2020).
2. Chloe Taylor (2020), "Here's why people are panic buying and stockpiling toilet paper to cope with coronavirus fears," CNBC, (Mar 11, 2020).
3. Scottie Andrew (2020), "The psychology behind why toilet paper, of all things, is the latest coronavirus panic buy," CNN, (Mar 9, 2020).
4. Veronika Job, Gregory M. Walton, Katharina Bernecker, and Carol S. Dweck, "Beliefs about willpower determine the impact of glucose on self-control," PNAS, 110: 37, (2013): 14837–14842.
5. Evan C. Carter and Michael E. McCullough "Publication bias and the limited strength model of self-control: has the evidence for ego depletion been overestimated?" *Frontiers in Psychology*, vol 5 (2014): 823.
6. Nir Eyal (2016) "Have We Been Thinking About Willpower the Wrong Way for 30 Years?" Havard Business Review, (November 2019).
7. Aditya Shukla (2020), "Construal Levels: Deliberate Creative Thinking Strategies & Hacks," *Cognition Today*, (February 26, 2020).
8. This was inspired by the brilliant work of The Neuroleadership Institute, led by David Rock at Microsoft
9. Jory MacKay, "This Brilliant Strategy Used by Warren Buffett Will Help You Prioritise Your Time," (2017) Inc.com.
10. Michael Bungay Stanier (2016) The Coaching Habit: Say Less, Ask More & Change the Way Your Lead Forever. Page Two
11. Timothy D. Wilson, David A. Reinhard, Erin C. Westgate, Daniel T. Gilbert, Nicole Ellerbeck, Cheryl Hahn, Casey L. Brown, and Adi Shaked, "Just Think: The Challenges of the Disengaged Mind," *Science* 345, issue 6192 (2014): 75– 7.
12. American Time Use Survey—2012 Microdata File, Bureau of Labor Statistics, U.S. Department of Labor, http://www.bls.gov/tus/datafiles_2012.htm.
13. K. Hsee, Adelle X. Yang, and Liangyan Wang, "Idleness Aversion and the Need for Justifiable Busyness," *Psychological Science* 21, no. 7 (July 2010): 926–30.

Chapter 4: *Together@Home*

1. Lisa F. Berkman, "The Role of Social Relations in Health Promotion," *Psychosomatic Medicine* 57, no. 3 (May–June 1995): 245–54.
2. Lisa F. Berkman and S. Leonard Syme, "Social Networks, Host Resistance, and Mortality: A Nine-year Follow-up Study of Alameda County Residents," *American Journal of Epidemiology* 109, no. 2 (February 1979): 186–204.
3. Jonathan Haidt, *The Happiness Hypothesis: Finding Modern Truth in Ancient Wisdom* (London: Arrow, 2007).
4. S. Cohen and T. B. Herbert, "Health Psychology: Psychological Factors and

Physical Disease from the Perspective of Human Psychoneuroimmunology," *Annual Reviews of Psychology* 47, no. 1 (1996): 113–42.

5. Ed Diener and Martin E. P. Seligman, "Very Happy People," *Psychological Science* 13, no. 1 (2002): 80–3.

6. Eva H. Telzer and Andrew J. Fuligni, "Daily Family Assistance and the Psychological Wellbeing of Adolescents From Latin American, Asian, and European Backgrounds," *Developmental Psychology* Vol. 45, No. 4, (2009): 1177–1189.

7. Eric J.Johnson* and Daniel Goldstein "Do defaults save lives?" *Science* 302 (2003): 1338–1339.

8. Jeremy B. Yorgason, Lee N. Johnson, Melanie S. Hill, Bailey Selland

9. "Marital Benefits of Daily Individual and Conjoint Exercise Among Older Couples," *Family Relations* 67: 2, (2018): 227–239.

10. Aron, A., Norman, C. C., Aron, E. N., McKenna, C., & Heyman, R. E., "Couples' shared participation in novel and arousing activities and experienced relationship quality," *Journal of Personality and Social Psychology*, 72(2), (2000): 273–284.

11. Kathleen D. Vohs, Yajin Wang, Francesca Gino, Michael I. Norton, "Rituals Enhance Consumption," *Psychological Science* 24, no. 9 (July 17, 2013): 1714–21.

12. Musick, K & Meier, A., "Assessing Causality and Persistence in Associations Between Family Dinners and Adolescent Wellbeing," *Journal of Marriage and Family* (2012).

13. Duke, MP., Fivush, R. Lazarus, A. & Bohanek, J., "Of Ketchup and Kin: Dinnertime Conversations as a Major Source of Family Knowledge, Family Adjustment, and Family Resilience." (2003).

14. Satter, E., *How to get your kid to eat . . . but not too much*, (Bull Publishing Co, 1987).

15. Smith LP, Ng SW, Popkin BM. "Trends in US home food preparation and consumption: analysis of national nutrition surveys and time use studies from 1965–1966 to 2007–2008," Nutr J 2013;12(1):45. 10.1186/1475-2891-12-45

16. Psychic entropy is a concept used in Mihaly Csikszentmihalyi, *Flow: The Classic Work on How to Achieve Happiness* (London: Rider/Random House, 1992).

17. Mihaly Csikszentmihalyi, *Flow: The Classic Work on How to Achieve Happiness* (London: Rider/Random House, 1992).

18. Fritz, C., Lam, C. F., & Spreitzer, G. M., "It's the little things that matter: An examination of knowledge workers' energy management," The Academy of Management Perspectives, 25(3), (2011): 28-39

19. John M. Darley and C. Daniel Batson, "'From Jerusalem to Jericho': A Study of Situational and Dispositional Variables in Helping Behaviour," *Journal of Personality and Social Psychology* 27, no. 1 (1973): 100–8.

20. https://www.itv.com/britaingettalking/the-campaign.html.

21. M.E.P. Seligman, T. A. Steen, N. Park, and C. Peterson, "Positive Psychology Progress: Empirical Validation of Interventions," *American Psychologist* 60, vol. 5 (July–August 2005): 410–21.

22. S. L. Gable, H. T. Reis, E. A. Impett, and E. R. Asher, "What Do You Do When Things Go Right? The Intrapersonal and Interpersonal Benefits of Sharing Positive Events," *Journal of Personality and Social Psychology* 87, no. 2 (2004): 228–45.

23. Holly B. Shakya and Nicholas A. Christakis (2017) "A New, More Rigorous Study Confirms: The More You Use Facebook, the Worse You Feel," *Harvard Business Review*, (April 10, 2020).

24. Robin Dunbar, "Neocortex Size as a Constraint on Group Size in Primates," *Journal of Human Evolution* 22, issue 6 (1992): 469–93.

25. Miller McPherson, Lynn Smith-Lovin, Matthew E. Brashears "Social Isolation in America: Changes in Core Discussion Networks over Two Decades," *American Sociological Review*, 71, (2006): 3.

26. Carolyn E. Schwartz, Janice Bell Meisenhelder, Yunsheng Ma, and George W. Reed, "Altruistic Social Interest Behaviours Are Associated with Better Mental Health," *Psychosomatic Medicine* 65, no. 5, 2003: 778–85.

27. Zoë Chance, Michael I. Norton "Giving Time Gives You Time,: *Psychological Science*, Vol 23, (2012): 10.

Chapter 5: *Commit@Home*

1. Gloria Mark, Victor Gonzalez, and Justin Harris, "No Task Left Behind? Examining the Nature of Fragmented Work," *Proceedings of the Conference on Human Factors in Computer Systems* (Portland, Oregon, 2005), 321–30.

2. Alia J. Crum and Ellen J. Langer, "Mind-set Matters: Exercise and the Placebo Effect," *Association for Psychological Science* 18, no. 2 (2007): 165–71.

3. Example given in Chip Heath and Dan Heath, *Switch: How to Change Things When Change Is Hard* (New York: Broadway Books, 2010).

4. Amy Arnsten cited in David Rock, *Your Brain at Work: Strategies for Overcoming Distraction, Regaining Focus, and Working Smarter All Day Long* (New York: HarperBusiness, 2009).

5. Rob Cross, Reb Rebele, Adam Grant (2016) "Collaborative Overload," *Harvard Business Review*, (January–February 2020).

6. Matthews, J. L.; Matlock, T, "Understanding the link between spatial distance and social distance", *Social Psychology*. 42 (3): (2011): 185–19.

7. Karen Sobel Lojeski (2015) "The Subtle Ways Our Screens Are Pushing Us Apart," *Harvard Business Review*, (January 2020).

8. Karen Sobel Lojeski (2015) "Hidden traps of virtual teams," HBR Webinar. https://hbr.org/webinar/2015/11/hidden-traps-of-virtual-teams Date?

9. Karen Sobel Lojeski (2015) Hidden traps of virtual teams. HBR Webinar. https://hbr.org/webinar/2015/11/hidden-traps-of-virtual-teams Date?

10. Gretchen Gavett (2014) "What People Are Really Doing When They're on a Conference Call," *Harvard Business Review*, (August 19, 2019).

11. Buehler, Roger; Dale Griffin; Michael Ross, "Exploring the "planning fallacy": Why people underestimate their task completion times". *Journal of Personality and Social Psychology*. 67 (3): (1994): 366–381.

12. E. Langer, A. Blank, and B. Chanowitz, "The Mindlessness of Ostensibly Thoughtful Action: The Role of 'Placebic' Information in Interpersonal Interaction," *Journal of Personality and Social Psychology* 36, no. 6 (1978): 639–42.

Chapter 6: *Think@Home*

1. Sunstein, C. R., "Nudging: A very short guide," *Journal of Consumer Policy*, 37(4), (2014): 583–588.

2. Teresa Amabile and Steven Kramer, *The Progress Principle: Using Small Wins to Ignite Joy, Engagement, and Creativity at Work* (Boston, MA: Harvard Business Review Press, 2011).

3. H. Pashler, J. C. Johnston, and E. Ruthruff, "Attention and Performance," *Annual Review of Psychology* 52 (February 2001): 629–51.

4. David Rock, *Your Brain at Work: Strategies for Overcoming Distraction, Regaining Focus, and Working Smarter All Day Long* (New York: Harper Business, 2009).

5. Melina Uncapher et al, "Media Multitasking and Cognitive, Psychological, Neural, and Learning Differences," *Pediatrics*, 140, (2017): S62-S66

6. Steven Kotler, "Create a Work Environment That Fosters Flow," *Harvard Business Review*, (October 11, 2019).

7. *Nakamura, J.; Csikszentmihályi, M.* "Flow Theory and Research". In C. R. Snyder Erik Wright, and Shane J. Lopez (ed.). *Handbook of Positive Psychology*. (Oxford University Press, 2001): 195–206.

8. D. F. Gucciardi and J. A. Dimmock, "Choking Under Pressure in Sensorimotor Skills: Conscious Processing or Depleted Attentional Resources?" *Psychology of Sport and Exercise* 9, issue 1 (January 2008): 45–59.

9. WHO Regional Office for Europe, "Burden of disease from environmental noise – Quantification of healthy life years lost in Europe," World Health Organization Report. (2011) https://www.who.int/quantifying_ehimpacts/publications/e94888/en/

10. Melanie Clay Wright, B Phillips-Bute, JB Mark, M Stafford-Smith, KP Grichnik, BC Andregg, JM Taekman, "Time of day effects on the incidence of anaethetic adverse events," *Quality and Safety in Health Care*, 15: 4; (2006): 258–63.

11. Hans Henrik Sievertsen, Francesca Gino, and Marco Piovesan, "Cognitive fatigue influences students' performance on standardized tests," PNAS, 113(10), (2016): 2621–2624.

12. Cindi May (2012) "The Inspiration Paradox: Your Best Creative Time Is Not When You Think," *Scientific American*. (May 2019).

13. Nicholas Bloom, James Liang, John Roberts, Zhichun Jenny Ying, "Does Working from Home Work? Evidence from a Chinese Experiment," The National Bureau of Economic Research, Working Paper No. 1887 (2013).

14. Gloria Mark, Victor Gonzalez and Justin Harris, "No Task Left Behind? Examining the Nature of Fragmented Work," *Proceedings of the Conference on Human Factors in Computer Systems* (Portland, Oregon, 2005), 321–30.

15. D. E. Meyer and D. E. Kieras, "A Computational Theory of Executive Cognitive Processes and Multiple-Task Performance: Part 1. Basic Mechanisms," *Psychological Review* 104, no. 1 (January 1997): 3–65.
    Also D. E. Meyer and D. E. Kieras, "A Computational Theory of Executive Cognitive Processes and Multiple-Task Performance: Part 2. Accounts of Psychological Refractory-Period Phenomena," *Psychological Review* 104, no. 1 (January 1997): 749–91.

16. S. Adam Brasel and James Gips, "Media Multitasking Behavior: Concurrent Television and Computer Usage," *Cyberpsychology, Behavior, and Social Networking* 14, no. 9 (2011): 527–34.

17. Gloria Mark, Victor Gonzalez, and Justin Harris, "No Task Left Behind? Examining the Nature of Fragmented Work," *Proceedings of the Conference on Human Factors in Computer Systems* (Portland, Oregon, 2005), 321–30.

18. Gloria Mark and Jennifer Robison, "Too Many Interruptions at Work?: Office Distractions Are Worse Than You Think—and Maybe Better," *Business Journal* (June 8, 2006), http://www.gallup.com/businessjournal/23146/Too-Many-Interruptions-Work.aspx.

19. D. T. de Ridder, G. Lensvelt-Mulders, C. Finkenauer, F. M. Stok, and R. F. Baumeister, "Taking Stock of Self-Control: A Meta-Analysis of How Trait Self-Control Relates to a Wide Range of Behaviours," *Personality and Social Psychology Review* 16, no. 1 (2012): 76–99.

Chapter 7: *Succeed@Home*

1. Alibaba Cloud (2020), "How Did Alibaba Help Retailer Lin Qingxuan Cope with the Coronavirus Outbreak?" (2020).

2. Martin Reeves, Nikolaus Lang and Philipp Carlsson-Szlezak (2020), "Lead Your Business Through the Coronavirus Crisis," *Harvard Business Review*, (February 27, 2020).

3. Joan Meyers-Levy and Rui (Juliet) Zhu, "The Influence of Ceiling Height: The Effect of Priming on the Type of Processing That People Use," *Journal of Consumer Research*, Vol. 34 (2007).

4. Manoj Thomas and Claire Tsai, "Psychological Distance and Subjective Experience: How Distancing Reduces the Feeling of Difficulty," *Journal of Consumer Research* (2011).

5. Ledgerwood, A., Trope, Y., & Chaiken, S.,"Flexibility Now, Consistency Later:

Psychological Distance and Construal Shape Evaluative Responding," *Journal of Personality and Social Psychology, 99*(1), (2010): 32–5.

6. Justin Berg, Jane Dutton, Amy Wrzesniewski, "What is job crafting and why does it matter," Michigan Ross School of Business; Theory to practice briefing, (2007).

7. Cited by Susan Adams, "The Test That Measures a Leader's Strengths," *Forbes. com* (August 28, 2009), http://www.forbes.com/2009/08/28/strengthsfinder-skills-test-leadership-managing-jobs.html.

8. Locke, Edwin A.; Latham, Gary P., "Building a practically useful theory of goal setting and task motivation: A 35-year odyssey," *American Psychologist.* 57 (9): (2002): 705–717.

9. Hamza Mudassir (2020), "COVID-19 Will Fuel the Next Wave of Innovation," https://www.entrepreneur.com/article/347669, (2020).

10. Mihaly Csikszentmihalyi, *Creativity: Flow and the Psychology of Discovery and Invention* (New York: Harper Perennial, 1997).

11. Kevin Coyne, Patricia Gorman Clifford and Renée Dye, "Breakthrough thinking inside the box," *Harvard Business Review,* (2007).

12. Aaron Glazer, "How Booking.com A/B Tests Ten Novenonagintillion Versions of its Site," https://blog.usejournal.com/how-booking-com-a-b-tests-ten-novenonagintillion-versions-of-its-site-25fc3a9e875b (2018).

13. Nicholas Bloom, James Liang, John Roberts, Zhichun Jenny Ying, "Does Working from Home Work? Evidence from a Chinese Experiment," The National Bureau of Economic Research, Working Paper No. 1887 (2013).

Chapter 8: *Evolve@Home*

1. Tom James (2011) "Black Death: The lasting impact," BBC History, (February 17, 2020).

2. "The End of Europe's Middle Ages: The Black Death,", at the Wayback Machine University of Calgary website, (Archived March 9, 2013).

3. Luthar SS. "Resilience in development: A synthesis of research across five decades," In: Cicchetti D, Cohen DJ, editors. Developmental Psychopathology: Risk, Disorder, and Adaptation. New York: Wiley; 2006: 740–795.

4. Tom Rath , *Vital Friends: The people you can't afford to live without,* (Gallup Press, 2006).

5. Sophie Scott (2020), "Laughter is a completely social phenomenon – we are 30 times more likely to laugh if there is someone else with us," *Science Focus*, sciencefocus.com (January 17, 2020).

6. W. Hofmann, R. F. Baumeister, G. Förster, and K. D. Vohs, "Everyday Temptations: An Experience Sampling Study of Desire, Conflict, and Self-Control," *Journal of Personality and Social Psychology* 102, no. 6 (2012): 1318–35.

7. Heidi Grant Halvorson (2020), The Science of Success: The If-Then Solution," *Psychology Today,* (June 9, 2020).

8. M. Bateson, D. Nettle, and G. Roberts, "Cues of Being Watched Enhance Cooperation in a Real-World Setting," *Biology Letters* (2006): 412–14.

9. Marshall Burke (2020) "COVID-19 reduces economic activity, which reduces pollution, which saves lives," Global Food, Environment and Economic Dynamics.